Modern Thought in Pain

The Frontiers of Theory

Series Editor: Martin McQuillan

Visit the Frontiers of Theory website at www.euppublishing.com/series/tfot

Modern Thought in Pain

Philosophy, Politics, Psychoanalysis

Simon Morgan Wortham

EDINBURGH
University Press

© Simon Morgan Wortham, 2015

Edinburgh University Press Ltd
The Tun – Holyrood Road
12 (2f) Jackson's Entry
Edinburgh EH8 8PJ
www.euppublishing.com

Typeset in 10.5/13 pt Sabon by
Servis Filmsetting Ltd, Stockport, Cheshire,
and printed and bound in Great Britain by
CPI Group (UK) Ltd, Croydon CR0 4YY

A CIP record for this book is available from the British Library

ISBN 978 0 7486 9241 5 (hardback)
ISBN 978 0 7486 9242 2 (webready PDF)

Contents

Series Editor's Preface

Since its inception Theory has been concerned with its own limits, ends and afterlife. It would be an illusion to imagine that the academy is no longer resistant to Theory but a significant consensus has been established and it can be said that Theory has now entered the mainstream of the humanities. Reaction against Theory is now a minority view and new generations of scholars have grown up with Theory. This leaves so-called Theory in an interesting position which its own procedures of auto-critique need to consider: what is the nature of this mainstream Theory and what is the relation of Theory to philosophy and the other disciplines which inform it? What is the history of its construction and what processes of amnesia and the repression of difference have taken place to establish this thing called Theory? Is Theory still the site of a more-than-critical affirmation of a negotiation with thought, which thinks thought's own limits?

'Theory' is a name that traps by an aberrant nominal effect the transformative critique which seeks to reinscribe the conditions of thought in an inaugural founding gesture that is without ground or precedent: as a 'name', a word and a concept, Theory arrests or misprisions such thinking. To imagine the frontiers of Theory is not to dismiss or to abandon Theory (on the contrary one must always insist on the it-is-necessary of Theory even if one has given up belief in theories of all kinds). Rather, this series is concerned with the presentation of work which challenges complacency and continues the transformative work of critical thinking. It seeks to offer the very best of contemporary theoretical practice in the humanities, work which continues to push ever further the frontiers of what is accepted, including the name of Theory. In particular, it is interested in that work which involves the necessary endeavour of crossing disciplinary frontiers without dissolving the specificity of disciplines. Published by Edinburgh University Press, in the city of Enlightenment, this series promotes a certain closeness to that spirit: the continued exercise of critical thought as an attitude of enquiry which counters modes of closed or conservative opinion. In this respect the series aims to make thinking think at the frontiers of theory.

Martin McQuillan

Acknowledgements

I have been grateful for the opportunity to present some of the material found in this book at a number of events and have benefited greatly from the input of a host of colleagues who attended them. Among these were the 2012 Spindel conference on 'Freudian Futures' hosted by the Philosophy Department at the University of Memphis organised by Pleshette deArmitt, the 2013 conference of the Society for Phenomenology and Existential Philosophy held at Kingston University with the support of the Centre for Research in Modern European Philosophy, the 2013 seminar series in the Department of English and Creative Writing at Lancaster University organised by Sharon Ruston, and the panel on 'Reading Language Capital' organised by Mauro Senatore and Ronald Mendoza-de Jesús convened as part of the annual meeting of the American Comparative Literature Association held in New York in March 2014. I would like to thank all those who invited me to these gatherings. Among those from whose engagement I have profited along the way, I would like to mention in particular Gil Anidjar, Elissa Marder, Pleshette deArmitt, Kas Saghafi, Simon Glendinning, Arthur Bradley, John Schad, Mick Dillon, Martin McQuillan, Etienne Balibar, Stella Sanford, Peter Hallward, Catherine Malabou, Peter Osborne, Tina Chanter and Andrew Benjamin. This book would simply not have been possible without the many exchanges I have enjoyed with colleagues in the Centre for Research in Modern European Philosophy and the London Graduate School at Kingston University. Finally, I would like to thank Jackie Jones at Edinburgh University Press for backing the project.

Part of Chapter 4 originally appeared as 'Time of Debt: On the Nietzschean origins of Lazzarato's indebted man', *Radical Philosophy*, 180 (2013), pp. 35–43. Chapter 5, 'Survival *of* Cruelty', was first published in the *Southern Journal of Philosophy*, 51, Spindel Supplement, (2013), pp. 126–41. I am grateful for the permission to reproduce this material.

Introduction: Modern Thought in Pain

Radical Evil

At the close of the twentieth century, perceived by many to have been among the most traumatic in history, and in the face of the most spectacular atrocity that seemed to announce new nightmares in its aftermath, a large number of books and articles devoted to the topic of evil were published by well-known academics working in the context of the continental or European tradition. Notable among these, as exemplary instances (though the list is long), were *Radical Evil: A Philosophical Interrogation* (2002) by Richard J. Bernstein (drafted in the period immediately prior to '9/11') and *The Idea of Evil* (2008) by Peter Dews, as well as Susan Neiman's prize-winning *Evil in Modern Thought* (2004). One could also point to a host of other volumes on the topic such as *Kant's Anatomy of Evil* (2010) edited by Sharon Anderson-Gold and Pablo Muchnik, or Anderson-Gold's own *Unnecessary Evil: History and Moral Progress in the Philosophy of Immanuel Kant* (2001). Of course, such titles are not exclusively the preserve of the twenty-first century: one thinks, for example, of Joan Copjec's collection, *Radical Evil*, from the mid-1990s, or Philippe Nemo's *Job and the Excess of Evil* (1978) as well as a number of other books connected with the upsurge of interest in ethics during that period, for instance Colin McGinn's *Ethics, Evil and Fiction* (1999).[1] Equally, it would be difficult not to think of many of the greatest contributions to modern European philosophy as connected in some way or other to questions of suffering, pain and torment that seem to form the legacy of the previous one hundred years. Here, certain names spring immediately to mind – Freud, Klein, Levinas, Adorno, Arendt – again, the list could go on – whose writings feature throughout the chapters that will follow. Arendt herself, of course, famously remarked in 1945 that: 'The problem of evil will be the fundamental question of postwar intellectual life in Europe.'[2] It is telling nevertheless that during the early years of the new millennium renewed interest in the question of evil, in particular as it might be construed in terms of the philosophical legacy post-Kant, both intensified and often reconstituted itself according to the (contested) forms of address demanded in the aftermath of '9/11'.

On certain occasions, then, the cultural and political climate of the early 2000s provoked some authors to speculate anew on the value philosophy might have in relation to contemporary human miseries and turmoil. In part, this was no doubt a reaction to widespread criticism meted out to the North American Humanities in particular, which in the wake of '9/11' were often publicly condemned as improperly equipped to reflect on the moral questions that '9/11' itself seemed to entail (beset as they had supposedly become by sundry forms of relativism, theoreticism, politically correct multiculturalism and so on). While it would be wrong to imply that more than a handful of subsequent interventions were opportunistic, and entirely proper instead to acknowledge the sincere motivation behind most writings on the topic, nevertheless it is important to recognise the different pathways that they took.

Susan Neiman's preface to the paperback edition of *Evil in Modern Thought*,[3] for instance, directly concerns itself with the aftermath of '9/11', which is acknowledged as forming its immediate context. (The book was originally drafted prior to this event.) Even though the precedence of this atrocity over other disasters, tragedies and outrages throughout the course of human history cannot be objectively gauged or asserted non-polemically, '9/11' is described nonetheless as 'a historical turning point that would change our discussion of evil' (p. xi). (A privileged example in Neiman's original book is the Lisbon earthquake of 1755, which she argues was a catastrophe of comparable proportions for the eighteenth century.) Neiman insists that it is foolhardy to imagine that philosophy might 'affect either terrorism or the worst reactions to it', yet she is confident nonetheless that by 'creating clarity, philosophy can offer moral orientation that helps sort out our reactions' to terrible situations of this type (p. xii). Political problems may well 'demand political solutions', as she puts it; but philosophy, so it seems, nevertheless forms an indispensable supplement to political judgement. If philosophy cannot issue a 'one-size-fits-all' explanation of evil, it has no less of a vital role to play in clarifying the problems to which 'evil' gives its name. And it seems a short leap here from philosophical to moral clarity, at any rate so far as Neiman is concerned.

In terms of reference to philosophical proper names, Arendt and Kant are specifically picked out in this handful of pages added to the original text (which itself concentrates on an array of writers and thinkers:

Leibniz, Pope, Rousseau, Kant, Hegel, Marx, Voltaire, Hume, Sade, Schopenhauer, Nietzsche, Freud, Camus, Arendt and so on), although their work is treated in a manner for which 'prefatory' would perhaps be the best euphemism. As Neiman hurriedly draws down the resources of the European philosophical tradition so as to pitch the question of philosophy's current value on the always uncertain trading floor of a preface (and – if one might slightly mix metaphors – a newly minted preface at that), the reader is left to wonder exactly how, after the 'turning point' of '9/11', philosophers like Kant are to be relied upon to provide philosophical clarity and, with it, moral orientation (beyond simply being 'clear' and hence 'moral', that is).

Peter Dews's *The Idea of Evil* starts out from Kant, with whom he engages with great rigour, but the effect is not to compensate for this deficit of explanation (one that seems all the more odd in Neiman's case given that for her philosophy is not just the discipline of the question, but a problem-solving activity). On the contrary, for Dews the very possibility both of philosophical clarity and rational interplay between philosophical reflection and moral action are precisely at issue in Kant. Dews examines the impact of Kant's notion of 'radical evil' upon the philosophical tradition that followed in his wake. (The principal text by Kant with which to concern ourselves here is *Religion within the Limits of Reason Alone* (1793).) He describes the consternation felt by some of Kant's most renowned peers when, against all expectations, Kant suggested that the evidence of our historical experience was out of kilter with contemporary philosophical optimism about the progress of civilisation towards a state of moral goodness. That human beings might be depicted in terms of a propensity to evil amounted to something of a challenge for Enlightenment thinkers. Some, like Schiller, interpreted Kant's remarks as a scandalous concession to the Christian doctrine of original sin (something that Kant himself explicitly contested). Others, like Reinhold, argued that by suggesting the inevitable shortcomings of man's moral efforts, Kant – recognising that rational faith could offer at best fragile proofs of divinity – had established instead the practical basis of belief as a firmer footing for religion in the period. Nevertheless, the idea that, as Dews puts it, 'human beings might be so constituted as to thwart progress towards the very goals that their own rational nature led them to strive for' (p. 22) was extremely unsettling for many of Kant's contemporaries, bequeathing to several of his most notable successors both deep-seated philosophical problems and new possibilities of thought. For, as Dews argues, such radical evil implies the 'inner diremption' (p. 22) of human freedom or 'will' as at once the basis for moral and immoral action. (We might note that in his book *Radical*

Evil, published six years earlier, Richard J. Bernstein's chapter on Kant follows a similar line of discussion to the one pursued by Dews here.) On the basis of this double conception of 'will' as an expression both of practical reason and power-of-choice that he finds in Kant, Dews cautions against understanding such a 'radical' propensity to evil merely in terms of a human 'nature'. Indeed, in his introduction Dews shrewdly points out how post-Kantian 'normative idealism', by understanding evil more simplistically than Kant as just a deplorable human lapse in moral standards, plays all too readily into the hands of 'its ostensible opponent, naturalism' which is usually 'only too ready to take the strain' (pp. 8–9). If the human 'will' has an innate tendency to choose against the moral law, evil is not done simply for evil's sake but is instead posited by Kant as a ground prior to every use of freedom in experience. For Dews, such thinking remains important if one is not to lapse into a certain interpretation of, let's say, the Holocaust as 'the paradigm of evil', whereby pure evil reveals itself as such by moving beyond mere 'self-interest' towards out-and-out 'nihilism', 'sheerly in order to violate the moral law . . . to demonstrate the superiority of the human will to any normative constraint' (p. 10). By forgoing the full implications of this dilemma of double 'will' (whereby evil may be postulated as a prior ground to the exercise of freedom, so that an ostensibly absolute departure from morality in fact proceeds from the same source as its very possibility) a 'misguided conception' of wickedness arises on the part of the 'good', encouraging 'naturalistic' conceptions of evil at odds with the more sophisticated predicament of thought that Dews detects in Kant's disquieting evocation of radical evil.

Ultimately, for Dews, Kantian thought can be imagined as an expression of the predicament of evil as much as a coherent or definitive philosophical interpretation of evil itself. He writes:

> Kant's attempt, unrivalled in its dignity and profundity, to combine a steadfast confidence in human progress with a disabused sense of the intractability of human evil, leads to philosophical perplexities which the appeal to rational faith does not alleviate, but simply intensifies. (p. 41)[4]

If from this perspective, post-Kantian philosophy establishes the conditions of possibility for a reformulation of religious notions of hope, 'no longer dependent on any specific dogma or revelation, but . . . inherent in our moral orientation to the world' (p. 13), as Dews muses in his introduction, it also bequeaths to us an idea of evil in which anticipation of the moral and practical defeat of wickedness vies uneasily with an awareness that the very idea of freedom – as a concept often closely allied to such anticipation – might serve as much to limit as to raise our expectations in this regard. If philosophy is to counter simplistic cultural and political discourses of 'evil' of the kind that were aggressively promoted by the Bush regime in the wake of '9/11', or if at any rate it might offer alternatives to them, then its departure from a self-identically given conception of 'freedom' (for instance, 'freedom' as the great adversary of 'evil' on a worldwide scale) marks a welcome resistance to crude polarities but also describes a certain tight spot from which philosophical thought after Kant struggles to extricate itself. (The anxiety of this predicament may be what led to swift condemnations of so-called postmodern relativism after '9/11', although this would be a displacement or projection not recognised by Dews, who is often happy to decry 'postmodern' thought in similarly sweeping terms – even, at one point, portraying it as the handmaiden to those forms of 'naturalism' he sees as profiting from the shortcomings of normative idealism post-Kant.[5]) Philosophy cannot establish a mere vantage point from which to adjudicate or resolve the question of evil or suffering, since it itself suffers from a degree of 'perplexity' that impedes, or at any rate intensely complicates, every attempt to 'alleviate' the malady that so affects or concerns it. To this extent, however, philosophy may participate in a problem in which it is not just interested but 'entangled', as Bernstein puts it, one that it must counteract or address not merely on behalf of others but for its own sake. If the (philosophical) predicament whereby evil can no more be simply banished from than easily reconciled with human 'will' in fact structures philosophy's relationship to human suffering or pain, then this constitutes an altogether ambivalent inheritance with which we must continue to grapple, however painful the struggle may be.

In fact, Bernstein more than once describes Kant's philosophy as 'entangled' in the midst of arguing, in a similar vein to Dews, that the possibility of evil does not derive from a defect in reason but exists as the prior ground of human freedom, yet such that it may nevertheless be considered a 'corruption of the will' (pp. 26–32). Thus 'radical evil' construed as a propensity not to follow the moral law is 'radically' rooted in the will's corruptibility, but it is 'woven' into human nature only as a basic feature of our freedom, so that we are to be considered responsible for the evil tendencies that are nonetheless endemic or innate to us, part of our free 'nature'. In these pages, Bernstein paints a picture of Kant's striving for philosophical coherence and integrity but also captures a sense of the tight spots into which he is driven by the thought of evil in its radical form. In thinking of how the problem of evil internally divides the 'human', as it were, 'Kant is at war with himself', as Bernstein puts it (p. 33). Once more, the entanglement of thought doesn't so much distance or drive it away from, as ensnare it *within*, the 'object' of philosophical concern.[6]

Bernstein's stance on Kant places him somewhere between the attitudes of Neiman and Dews. He suggests that the answer to the question of 'whether Kant's reflections on evil, especially radical evil, can help to guide our thinking about the evil we have witnessed in the twentieth century' is necessarily 'a mixed one' (pp. 42–3). Yet his ultimate claim, that Kant's emphasis on personal responsibility remains relevant since it demands of us a morality without alibi, falters (or rather resonates with the Kantian predicament) not simply because it fails to take the measure of modern evils, but because it surely begins to unravel once the origin of moral choices is acknowledged as 'inscrutable'. It is almost as if that which must justify itself is itself unjustifiable, as if the argument cannot help becoming entangled.

Theodicy

In a footnote to his essay 'Useless Suffering',[7] Emmanuel Levinas extends his critique of theodical interpretations of evil by alluding to Kant's short treatise, 'On the Failure of All the Philosophical Attempts at a Theodicy' (1791),[8] which for Levinas demonstrates the 'theoretical weakness' of arguments in favour of a theodical approach to the question of evil and suffering.[9] Kant's text, appearing two years before his 'radical evil' thesis, opens by way of a highly orchestrated juridical process whereby theodicy is set before 'the tribunal of reason' (p. 283) – a scene followed, later in the text, by Kant's reflections on the trial of Job, which reasserts the constraints of reason evoked from the very beginning. Alongside Kant's preference for a faith based on morality rather than vice versa, then, we find here a philosophical attitude that, in regard to the exchanges between Job and his friends, favours 'honesty in the avowal of the powerlessness of our reason' over self-interested, subtle or insincere 'reasoning' (p. 294). In this text, Kant also asserts that 'mortal man' is ultimately unable to attain knowledge of the 'moral wisdom of the Creator of the World' since he is incapable of establishing in the world of experience a concept to unite 'artistic' and 'moral wisdom' (combining understanding of the arrangement of the world with a sense of its creator's perfection) so as to found theoretical knowledge of a higher 'good'. Furthermore, if subtle 'reasoning' is here linked to the insincerity that is 'the principal affliction of human nature', the depiction of a sincere character, such as Job, is not just 'edifying' but 'moving' – perhaps saddening and painful, too – since it conveys the 'property farthest removed from human nature' (p. 296). If the problem of evil (and, for that matter, the question of what is by contrast edifying in the sincere character of Job) surpasses and confounds conventional religious interpretation of the kind offered by Job's comforters, it also recalls reason's limitations once more. Indeed, a degree of difficulty necessarily arises to the extent that, as much as reason can be used to demonstrate the irredeemable failings of theodicy, its limits unavoidably reduce our capacity to, as it were, objectively assess theodical claims. As much as reason can be deployed so as to contribute to a general weakening of those arguments that rationalise suffering from a religious point of view, ultimately it is the 'pious humility' of a sincere Job and not the slippery 'speculative reason' of his friends that may be opposed to theodicy, in order to more fully expose its failings from, as it were, a moral rather than a purely theological or philosophical point of view. Bernstein reads Kant's text as follows:

> Kant is declaring that theodicy is not a task of science, but a matter of faith. If theodicy is conceived as a *science* or a discipline that can yield *theoretical knowledge*, then it is *impossible*. Consequently, not only do all attempted philosophical theodicies fail; they *must* fail. (pp. 3–4)

Hence, 'Kant is the modern philosopher who initiates the inquiry into evil without specific recourse to philosophical theodicy' or the claim of 'some theoretical *knowledge* . . . of God' (p. 4); but who instead imagines an 'authentic' – as Kant himself puts it (p. 293) – faith-based theodicy where faith is an expression or condition of morality rather than vice versa. If, as Bernstein argues, the 'specter of theodicy still casts its shadow' on philosophy after Kant (p. 4) – for instance, in the theodical aspects of Hegel's dialectical thought, whereby, as Bernstein puts it, 'we come to see evil as a necessary stage in the becoming of Absolute Spirit' (p. 100)[10] – it is therefore important to note that part of the reason for this may be that, in the aftermath of Kant's thought, it is no easy matter for philosophy to just 'trump' theodicy, to simply outdo or surpass it, and thus consign it forever to the ash can of philosophical history. Just as, in the 'radical evil' thesis, Kantian thought cannot help but become entangled in the problem of its own concern, since the nature of that entanglement is somewhat endemic in terms of the project it sets itself, so in his attempt to disparage the theodical impulse Kant, by acknowledging the limits of reason, suggests the philosophical constraints within which such a gesture necessarily operates.[11]

Playing no doubt knowingly upon religious language, 'Useless Suffering' speaks of theodicy as a persistent 'temptation', a central 'component of the self-consciousness of European humanity' (at any

rate 'up to the trials of the twentieth century' (p. 96)). Such a 'temptation' might be traced, for instance, through Kant's '*practical* need to
postulate a beneficent God' (in Bernstein's terms (p. 169)) as the
perhaps fraught counterpart of his criticism of theodicy as a theoretical
problem. Levinas's essay can be read against the broader backdrop of
modern philosophical assertions of suffering's meaninglessness, which
one might associate with the advent of the various forms of atheistic or
psychologistic thought often linked to figures like Schopenhauer,
Nietzsche and Freud (although it is debatable how far any such thought,
suffering as it may do from 'meaninglessness' or at any rate the diremption of meaning and being, in fact dispenses convincingly with the
redemptive impulse).[12] Levinas starts out by arguing that, if suffering is
'a *datum* in consciousness', it is simultaneously 'unassumable', and as
such features in 'consciousness' in spite of consciousness itself (p. 91).
Suffering is unassumable, not because of its excessive sensory intensity,
but because pain offers irreducible violence to the 'dimensions of
meaning that seem to open themselves to it'. Suffering is therefore,
among other things, the name we might give to a certain incapacity to
assemble 'data into a meaningful whole', a disturbance of consciousness within its own operations, or in other words a modality of consciousness in which it experiences itself as just this disturbance.
(Similarly, in Levinas's essay 'Transcendence and Evil', the transcendence of evil is suggested in the sense that it cannot be fully integrated,
comprehended or synthesised: indeed, that is its very experience.) The
refusal or resistance of meaning in suffering, therefore, precisely affects
the 'datum' in question (pp. 91–2). Suffering is in-spite-of-conscious-
ness in the further sense that, as the unassumable, it cannot be dealt
with as the result of conscious agency or will. Indeed, the profound
passivity engendered by suffering is so fundamental, so original, that it
cannot be reassimilated to the conceptual schema of the 'active' and the
'passive'. By extension, suffering is radically prior to the 'receptivity of
the senses' if construed according to unquestioned notions of 'active
reception' or immediate perception (p. 92). However, it is not simply
the case that suffering as 'pure undergoing' divests consciousness of a
certain freedom by reducing the human being to the status of a merely
passive 'thing'. For suffering occurs more 'irremissibly' than as just an
oppositional pole or force which confronts and threatens to overwhelm
'active' being. The question, then, is not of the 'non-freedom' inflicted
upon being by suffering (compare here the Kantian interplay between
the exercise of freedom and the intrinsic possibility of evil), but rather
of the non-meaning or 'un-meaning' of suffering which it must confront
as a profound impasse. And yet suffering in its very meaninglessness, its

non-integratable excess (indeed its non-dialecticisability between Good and Evil), opens the possibility of the ethical – beyond theodicy, beyond freedom construed as autonomy – insofar as it entails what Levinas terms the 'original call for aid' (p. 93). Even the most debilitating sense of abandonment, solitude and isolation brought about by the experience of utterly inexpressible pain leaves this call undimmed. To suffer suffering, to endure the utterly useless and unjustifiable suffering of the other, gives rise to the possibility of ethical response (albeit a possibility that leads beyond the simple adoption in good conscience of 'active' programmes, initiatives, policies, laws and moralities of all sorts, designed to ameliorate suffering in a planned way – however necessary they may also be), thereby opening up what Levinas describes as the radically ethical perspective of the 'interhuman'.[13]

For Levinas, then, various attempts to discern, explicate or commend pain's meaning – whether in the field of religious or social thought, in the practice of education or morality, or in the exercise of legal 'justice', etc. – must come down to a certain theodicy at work once more. Since theodicy is tasked with resolving the problem of evil by reconciling the occurrence of worldly suffering in all its manifestations with an overriding belief in ultimate goodness (be it that of God, Nature, History or whatever), in such terms pain becomes not just senseless and gratuitous but instead comprehensible and bearable. As we have remarked, Levinas calls such theodicy a constant 'temptation', yet what from him is most striking about the twentieth century in particular is the 'destruction of all balance' (p. 97) between the persistence of theodical thought and feeling, on the one hand, and, on the other, the extreme and horrifying evils on a planetary scale which would seem to test beyond limit the theodical imagination. If Levinas speaks of an 'end' to theodicy, still we must be attentive to what this entails. Amid the worst evils of the twentieth century, pain 'in its undiluted malignancy, suffering for nothing . . . renders impossible and odious every proposal and every thought that would explain it' in theodical terms (p. 98). And yet, at the same time, to the extent that this 'end of theodicy' renders starkly apparent the wholly unjustifiable suffering of the other – a suffering that we cannot but suffer – it provokes the ethical perspective of the 'interhuman' that Levinas goes on to consider. However, the problem of the end of theodicy is also that the question of a 'human morality of goodness' no doubt has some afterlife beyond theodicy's demise, albeit one which, by viewing the 'justification of the neighbor's pain' as 'the source of all immorality' (p. 99), seeks to surpass every theodical perspective. In other words, if 'goodness' is the upshot of theodicy, it is also difficult to imagine the survival of the ethical perspective without reference to it in some form or other (even, for instance, through allusion to the 'immorality' of theodical interpretation).

In relation to the twentieth-century fate of the Jews, Levinas poses the related problem: 'To renounce after Auschwitz this God absent from Auschwitz – no longer to assure the continuation of Israel – would amount to finishing the criminal enterprise of National Socialism' (p. 99). The question of the absolutely senseless suffering at Auschwitz which signals the end of theodicy thus calls us to think how Levinasian ethics might survive its ruins,[14] living on without it, without being destroyed in turn by theodicy's very 'end'. As Dews puts it, in the last lines of his own chapter on Levinas, the 'unconditional pressure' of the 'ethical demand' so stridently asserted by Levinasian thought risks becoming drained 'of all meaning' at the point any 'glimmer of confidence in the goodness of the world' disappears after Auschwitz (p. 182): drained of meaning, not in the sense of persisting as an ethics beyond theodicy, but in the sense of becoming rather pointless or senseless *as* an ethics, being already defeated, if all goodness is henceforth impossible. Thus, Dews writes:

> Those who blithely defend Levinas . . . affirming that here – at last – is an ethics without false compensations, without theodicy, overlook the fact that Levinas is far too subtle and sensitive a thinker not to have pondered intensely over these issues. (p. 176)

Here, then, for Dews, the fact that the ethical upshot of 'useless suffering' exists in a deeply pained relation to its very ethical possibility remains a troubling feature of Levinas's thought.

Towards the end of his essay, Levinas thus speaks of 'a new modality in the faith of today, and even in our moral certitudes' (p. 100), one he ties, here and elsewhere, to the Jewish faith as an eschewal of the ensemble of ideas one would associate with theodicy. (I explore further this aspect of Levinas's writings in the final section of the third chapter of this book, 'Distress II'.) To the extent that this assertion moves us in a somewhat Kantian direction, it once more calls for thinking about the secular or social world as much as the religious sphere, which must be remade if 'useless suffering' is not to utterly overwhelm 'faith' or 'meaning' in a way that signals the ultimate redundancy of ethics. Here, it is clear that the notion of the interhuman does not simply proceed from, nor limit itself to, the classical paradigm – State, Society, City, Law – which 'establishes mutual obligations between citizens' (p. 100). The interhumanity demanded by 'useless suffering' is thus not posed simply in terms of the coexistence of already constituted consciousnesses or subjectivities made to interact along the given horizon of political order, since, as Levinas has already suggested, the interhuman in its most decisive possibility doesn't just precede, exceed or resist the proposition and prospect of a unified, autonomous consciousness, but by extension questions the very hypothesis of a replete community bound together by some theodical telos. Thus no 'social determinism' or 'common destiny' can guarantee the interhuman. The 'order of politics' is 'neither the sufficient condition nor the necessary outcome of ethics' (p. 100). Instead, the radical 'non-indifference' or responsibility of each to another that 'useless suffering' demands is the enduring test of all conditioned reciprocities, and not their upshot. It is the excess of all human commerce and exchange rather than a 'civil' consequence. As Levinas puts it, 'the pure altruism of this responsibility inscribed in the ethical position of the *I qua I* . . . is prior to any contract that would specify precisely the moment of reciprocity – a point at which altruism and disinterestedness may, to be sure, continue, but at which they may also diminish or die out' (p. 100). What remains to be thought, on this basis, is just this *I qua I* as distinct from an empirical subject, a discrete psychological consciousness or a socio-political citizen in the classical sense, an *I qua I* made (ethically) possible, however seemingly impossible this may be, by the useless suffering of the other – which is to say, by an asymmetrical relation to the other founded on 'alterity' prior to 'reciprocity' (p. 101).[15] Later in the book, we will examine Lyotard's conception of civil life as tied to the other-human/other-than-human, suggesting that it opens a pathway between an ethics-of-the-other position of this type and a rethinking of the grounds of the 'civil' that exceeds and unsettles the classical paradigm evoked by Levinas, coming closer perhaps to his understanding of what the 'interhuman' may be. (In this, Lyotard's position cannot easily be assimilated either by cruder forms of defence or critique of the classical concepts and models of citizenship.)

With Levinas, then, even the seemingly barest evocation of theodicy's end, and hence of suffering's meaninglessness, cannot help but *suffer* meaninglessness in the sense of enduring a philosophically pained relationship to it. From Kant to Levinas, the relationship of modern thought to pain, in other words, is one in which we continually witness modern thought *in* pain, perhaps even *as* pain (as this all too brief and necessarily partial introduction has begun to show). This continues to the present day. Some, like Žižek, recuperate such pain (in his case, via the figure of Christ) as the origin of emancipatory possibility, while others, like Rancière, tend to dismiss pain as the predisposition of a mournful, melancholic ethics that, in demanding ethical consensuality based on the irredeemable suffering of the past, blocks future emancipation. In this regard, the double gesture of the chapters that follow is to affirm the pain of modern thought post-Kant, while seeking conceptions of its *possibility* that neither correspond with the revolutionary embrace of Žižek nor concur with the political dismissal of Rancière. Here, I revisit the thought of figures like Levinas and Lyotard – frequently the object of, as it were, post-poststructuralist dissatisfaction with an ethics-of-the-other position – in order to evaluate what surpluses such philosophical resources may still yield in the wake of their repeated rejection or silencing. In this, I do not aim so much to rehabilitate these figures by defending the consistency or cogency of their thought as to recognise in such rejections further examples of what I am calling modern thought in pain (a 'pain' that, as we've already seen, is not merely symptomatic of difficulties 'internal' to philosophy, but that frequently intensifies as its limits are reached, its thresholds tested, its conditions of possibility opened up, its relations questioned, its borders breached).

The context for Chapter 1, 'After Pains', is the interwar years of the twentieth century – a moment, perhaps, when the sense of a crisis of modernity was most intensely felt and debated. The feeling of extreme national humiliation in Germany led to the historical experience of *Nachkriege* or 'afterwar', one that was characterised not only by a devastating sense of loss but more radically by a refusal to accept the war's ending, in particular on the part of the German Right. In this respect, *Nachkriege* acquires a double and contradictory meaning. Looking at the emergence of what may be termed reactionary modernism in Germany during this time, the far-right elements of which set the scene for the rise of German fascism, I examine the writings of Ernst Jünger, particularly his essay 'On Pain', and the reception of such work in the interwar years. Reactionary modernism makes its case on the strength of a retrospective affirmation of a heroic past, yet devotes itself to a futural project that, it can be argued, is highly modernistic in many respects. To the extent that it endeavours to resist the modernistic temporality in which it is also grounded, reactionary modernism is formed by a contradiction that is constitutive of its own conditions of possibility. Reactionary modernism must therefore embrace performatively that which it seeks to overcome or supersede: modernity itself. I argue that the name Jünger gives to this (modernistic) experience of contradiction – *Nachkriege* itself – is pain. Moreover, I contrast two important readings of Jünger, one found in Walter Benjamin's 1930 essay, 'Theories of German Fascism', the other undertaken in Leo Strauss's 1940 lecture, 'The Living Issues of German Postwar Philosophy'. Benjamin interprets Jünger's work as an effect of the 'afterwar' repression of loss, the constitutive contradictions of which might nevertheless be reworked into the conditions for social transformation. Strauss explains Jünger's influence in terms of a crisis of historical consciousness, that of historicism, handed down from the Enlightenment. For Strauss this crisis necessitates a return to classical antiquity as the scene of a 'natural' philosophy that is more original than the historicist versions that blight historical civilisation. Thus, between Benjamin and Strauss, we find ourselves once more in the wake of the 'double-time' that constitutes reactionary modernism in the first place. While neither Benjamin nor Strauss accept 'pain' on the terms of Jünger's own analysis, both in their very different ways recognise that his thought on the topic is itself 'pained': that is to say, they treat it as the symptom of a certain malady or ailment. For both, however, the remedy will unavoidably involve some more pain: for Strauss, access to 'natural' philosophy is presented as far from a serene prospect, in the sense that it necessitates yet more thoroughgoing historicisation of the historicism that in other ways afflicts us (a project that has barely yet been imagined); for Benjamin, to the extent that the possibility of radical social change rests upon the transformation of an experience of defeat that is currently shrouded in denial, the future depends on a more thoroughgoing assumption of loss.

The subsequent two chapters move us towards a more recent set of philosophical debates and texts, whose climate may nonetheless be understood in terms of the aftermath of the 'next war' that looms over Benjamin's essay. Central to this part of the book is my attempt to take issue with Rancière's depiction of an ethics-of-the-other position as a paralysing form of melancholia that obstructs the potentiality of emancipation. Rancière's critique in this regard is often focused on the writings of Jean-François Lyotard, although it is undoubtedly a larger swipe at those traditions of thought, like poststructuralism, that stand to one side of the Marxist legacy. The thrust of Rancière's argument suggests that the relationship of such thought to the traumatic experiences of the Second World War is akin to that of German reactionary modernism in regard to the First World War as analysed by Benjamin in the interwar years, namely a refusal to move beyond the pain of loss and mourning and thus a refusal of truly emancipatory possibility. 'Distress I' examines Rancière's critique of Lyotard's interpretation of the sublime. (Here, it should be noted, Lyotard's reading of the Kantian sublime links to Lyotard's own suggestion that thought for Kant is always somehow thought in pain.) Rancière's wider dissatisfaction with Lyotard hangs on a recursive reference to a lecture given by Lyotard for Amnesty International in 1993, 'The Other's Rights', a text that Rancière fails to read with any rigour. My purpose here, however, is less to restore a 'correct' reading of this text than it is to use Lyotard's lecture as the occasion to ask questions about the nature of Rancière's animosity towards him. I argue that, since on closer inspection Lyotard's discourse in this lecture cannot be reduced to Rancière's image of postmodern thought as paralysed by mystical reverence for a primordial Other which produces itself as melancholic obstacle to the onward march of political emancipation, we must read his hostility 'otherwise'. In fact, it much more comes down to a dispute between equality and dissymmetry as the founding term of the possibility of human relationships. Be that as it may, I ask whether the relationship of Rancière to Lyotard is to be understood in terms of the 'distress' of the differend which impedes any common ground between them (which, ironically enough, may echo the radical dissymmetry of instruction and address that in his 1993 Amnesty lecture Lyotard discerns as the formative 'distress' of entry into civil life, or of the other-human/other-than-human), or whether it is to be thought of in terms of the pained agitation occasioned by *différance* (that is, of a differentiation between the two which cannot fully repress a certain deferral, and thus a more complex interconnection). The 'distress' I detect underlying Rancière's position is also, I argue, ultimately that of a desire to resist the sublime as effectively a pure impediment to emancipatory politics, a desire which knows it threatens to delegimitise other aspects of Rancière's own project and analysis. Here, I point out the double gesture on Rancière's part of, on the one hand, a refutation of the sublime (as) blockage itself, and, on the other, a semi-repressed inclusion of the sublime within a 'Schillerian' aesthetics of emancipation that he advocates.

'Distress II' picks up afresh the question of whether the contrast between Rancière's emphasis on human equality and Lyotard's accent on dissymmetry can really be reduced to a matter of straightforward opposition. By exploring the possibility of certain connections between the economy and practice of masochism described by Deleuze and the formation of civil life in the Lyotardian 'text', I aim to show that Deleuze's depiction of masochism's desire to educate the other corresponds in significant ways with Lyotard's image of the 'Other' as master-teacher. By way of this comparison I try to complicate overly simplistic distinctions between the 'distressing' instruction of such an 'Other' and the emancipatory teaching of the Rancièrian ignorant schoolmaster, since the master-teacher who for Lyotard forms a couple with the distressed *infantia* at the origin of civil life is much less the 'knowing', forceful stultifier at the heart of the explicatory tradition so disparaged by Rancière than he is a potentially transformative educator found at the always divisible borders of what both masochism and emancipation might mean and do.

Moving away somewhat from Lyotard and Rancière, the chapter goes on to explore some of the writings of Slavoj Žižek. Rather like Rancière, Žižek advocates a departure from what he sees as some of the depoliticising constraints of ethical thought, abandoning certain poststructuralist conceptions of difference linked to 'respect for the other' in favour of an idea of difference that, for him, potentialises radically egalitarian unification via a collective politics that is highly suspicious of 'PC' ideas about diversity and pluralism. Interestingly, though, while Rancière clearly disdains Lyotardian evocations of pain, Žižek's political project – particularly in its politico-theological or Christological aspects – is frequently put forth in terms of the radical value of pain. Indeed, one might wonder if this divergence, wherein the origin and the obstacle to emancipation are given practically the same name, isn't itself potentially rather painful for the emancipatory project of recent theory. Through reading several texts by Žižek, including the writings found in *God in Pain*, I argue that a series of pained distinctions between Christianity, Judaism and Islam complicate Žižek's insistence upon the radical specificity of the Christian as granting special access to revolutionary possibility. The chapter concludes with a reading of Levinas's postwar writings on Léon Brunschvicg. Here, Levinas effectively speaks against, and not for, that assemblage of ideas with which Rancière suggests the ethics-of-the-other position is inextricably connected. The sacred or the mystical (or, put differently, a feeling of redemptive entitlement) is no more pandered to, than a sense of war is oppressively or 'traumatically' retained. In fact, such ideas are to be resisted, not embraced, if we are not to be dominated by the horrors of the past. As Levinas puts it, Brunschvicg's is 'a profound text', 'not because it involves the extrinsic witness of history, but because it denounces the very ambiguity of exaltation'.[16]

Given Rancière's dissatisfaction with the idea of an irredeemable indebtedness that constitutes the ethics-of-the-other position he so derides, it is interesting that certain brands of Marxism have come to associate neoliberalism with a debt capitalism that has the future in an inescapable stranglehold, to the point of its effective cancellation as such. Here, one might point to Maurizio Lazzarato's 'indebted man' thesis, which in its polemical thrust hardly questions this idea that we are now saddled with unrepayable debts. My next chapter therefore looks at recent writings on debt, notably those by Lazzarato and David Graeber. In terms of the latter, I ask whether his book *Debt: The First 5,000 Years* is able to resist the insidious logic of a retroactive interpretation of debt that it is devoted to overturning. Throughout his wide-ranging discussion of debt, credit, money and power across five millennia and an array of empires and nations, I argue that Graeber's double and divided narrative of historical origins and development is perhaps just as retroactive as the 'origin stories' he wishes to oppose. I point out certain tensions and contradictions in Graeber's book that have to do with unresolved theoretical questions at his thesis's core. These problems undermine Graeber's attempt (via an empiricist method of anthropological example) to break free from the retroactive explanations that he reductively projects in terms of the figure of disciplinary economics. As the chapter turns to Lazzarato, the influence upon his work of Nietzsche's conception of debt is recognised. But through a rereading of Nietzsche, two objections arise to Lazzarato's thesis. First, his notion of a catastrophic future-without-future of unending debt relies upon an understanding of the ever-intensifying asymmetry of power that elevates the creditor to near-Godlike status. While this suggestion may derive from a strand of Nietzschean thought in the *Genealogy of Morals*, the further implication of a debt so all-pervasive that it leaves no creditor intact opens up the possibility of rigorous thinking about the non-self-identical or divisible limits of sovereignty and sovereign debt (an opportunity Lazzarato does not pursue). Second, despite some of the more dominant flourishes of his remarks in the *Genealogy*, one can excavate from Nietzsche the idea that the retroactivity so pivotal to the very possibility of debt is based on a false continuity between past and present, 'origin' and 'aim', which implies in turn that debt itself aggresses against temporal continuity in general. As such, debt's ostensible sponsorship of neoliberalism's violence against all future time itself becomes questionable and indeed resistible. Recent writings that assess the pain of debt – whether or not they subscribe to the idea, often traced through Nietzsche, of debt's indebtedness to pain itself[17] – are, therefore, themselves somewhat pained by its very idea.

The next chapter in the book turns to the idea of cruelty. At a certain point in its lengthy development, Derrida's essay 'Psychoanalysis Searches the States of Its Soul' – which among other things reflects on the seemingly pervasive nature of human cruelty – makes a distinction between Nietzsche and Freud, whereby the latter maintains an 'opposable term' to cruelty, however impossible it may seem. The chapter explores the status and significance of this 'opposable term' for thinking about the survival of cruelty in Derridean terms, and in a postscript carries its reading into the question of the 'side of life' and of death in Derrida's *H. C. for Life*. The book closes with a short essay on Melanie Klein in which the question of what may survive is once more critical. It is Klein whose writings for Julia Kristeva confirm Proust's assertion that 'ideas come to us as the substitutes for griefs'. Klein charts the passage, during early infancy, from the psychotic-schizoid to the depressive position. This represents an attempt to overcome, through a process of integration, an original set of object-relations in which the other and the self are radically fragmented. For Kristeva, it is by generating the resources for language and thinking, grounded in the capacity for the symbolisation of an object, that this movement confirms Proust's contention. My essay explores the potential for dark humour within Klein's often somewhat bleak writings and poses the question of its possible limits. Turning to one of her very last essays, on loneliness, I argue that it is our loneliness – in a Kleinian sense – that may outlive us, even and perhaps especially in the creative works we undertake in order to confront it. As Derrida's essay on cruelty suggests, modern thought may be in pain even beyond any opposition between life and death.

Notes

1. Bibliographical details of these texts are as follows: Richard J. Bernstein, *Radical Evil: A Philosophical Interrogation* (Cambridge: Polity Press, 2002); Peter Dews, *The Idea of Evil* (Oxford: Blackwell, 2008); Susan Neiman, *Evil in Modern Thought: An Alternative History of Philosophy* (Princeton: Princeton University Press, 2004); *Kant's Anatomy of Evil*, ed. Sharon Anderson-Gold and Pablo Muchnik (Cambridge: Cambridge University Press, 2010); Sharon Anderson-Gold, *Unnecessary Evil: History and Moral Progress in the Philosophy of Immanuel Kant* (New York: SUNY Press, 2001); *Radical Evil*, ed. Joan Copjec (London: Verso, 1996); Philippe Nemo, *Job and the Excess of Evil* (Pittsburgh: Duquesne Press, 1978); Colin McGinn, *Ethics, Evil and Fiction* (Oxford: Oxford University Press, 1999). Another title worthy of mention is *Rethinking Evil*, ed. Maria Pia Lara (Berkeley and Los Angeles: California University Press, 2001). Further page references to these texts, where they arise, will be given in the main body of the chapter.
2. Hannah Arendt, 'Nightmare and Flight', in *Hannah Arendt: Essays in Understanding, 1930–1954*, ed. Jerome Kohn (New York: Harcourt, Brace & Co., 1994), p. 134.
3. This book originally appeared in 2002, being drafted before '9/11', with a paperback edition coming out in 2004 that included a new preface seeking to grapple with this event. By that time, the book had won (among other prizes) the Association of American Publishers Award for Best Professional/ Scholarly Book in Philosophy. Further page references to Nieman's book will be given in the main body of the chapter.
4. In *Radical Evil*, Richard J. Bernstein says something similar about Kant's somewhat ambivalent stance: 'Kant seeks to walk a fine line. On the one hand, he is skeptical of the idea of moral progress whereby human beings can (and will) achieve moral perfection. On the other hand, although human beings can never escape from the propensity to evil . . . there can be

moral progress in history insofar as human beings can become actually good by virtue of their freedom. Kant's faith in (limited) moral and political progress is played out against a dark background, a realistic appraisal of "crooked humanity".' Bernstein goes on to argue that Kant's conception of radical evil is beset by 'tensions and problems' that stem from the difficulties of reconciling the possibilities of human good and evil (p. 20).

5. See *The Idea of Evil*, p. 9.

6. Bernstein further argues that Kant is unable to offer a 'deduction' or proof that, on his own terms, would be needed in order to justify the universal claims of the radical evil thesis, and instead presents empirical observations which leave something of an 'inscrutable' abyss at the explanatory core of the problem.

7. Emmanuel Levinas, 'Useless Suffering', in *Entre Nous: On Thinking-of-the-Other*, trans. Michael B. Smith and Barbara Harshav (London: Athlone, 1998), pp. 91–101. Further references to this text will be included in the main body of my chapter.

8. This text is included as an appendix in Michel Despland's *Kant on History and Religion*, trans. the author (Montreal and London: McGill-Queen's University Press, 1973), pp. 283–97, to which my own chapter will refer in terms of specific citations included henceforth in its main body.

9. This reference is to the essay's footnotes found on pp. 240–2 of *Entre Nous*.

10. It may be interesting to note that Dews book has a chapter on what he terms Hegel's 'wry philosophy'.

11. One could read such claims further alongside Dews's book, particularly as it moves from Fichte, Schelling and Hegel to the thought of Schopenhauer and Nietzsche. Here, Dews reminds us that the course taken by post-Kantian idealism suggests that simply 'to think of evil and suffering as posing a problem for a *pre-existing* belief in God may not be the most illuminating way of viewing the matter' (p. 119), not least since what is at stake in idealism post-Kant is how to rethink the intersection of faith, reason and morality from a philosophical point of view. I mention this to underscore the fact that, instead of there being simply a decisive moment of argument in philosophy's treatment of the problem of evil, there is instead something of a pained history.

12. Dews's book includes a chapter that concentrates on Schopenhauer and Nietzsche, interestingly subtitled 'suffering from meaninglessness', as if the perceived meaninglessness of suffering was, or is, itself a source of suffering. Dews well appreciates that Schopenhauer thinks of post-theistic morality, with which we cannot dispense, as still reliant on a '*metaphysical* conception of the world' in terms of which it becomes meaningful (p. 125). Thus he cites Sebastian Gardner's image of Schopenhauer as challengingly caught between a rationalist humanism and a scientific naturalism still in the pay of metaphysics, the latter provoking Nietzschean critique, notably in terms of the perceived connection between Schopenhauerian 'will' and original sin (albeit a critique that Nietzsche himself cannot be wholly exempted from, in the sense that for Nietzsche the doctrine of original sin is itself the original sin, as Stephen Mulhall, cited here by Dews, has argued). Once more, a pained philosophical history seems in evidence (see

note 11 above) – Dews concludes his chapter by suggesting the redemptive impulse of Nietzschean thought.

13. Relatedly, Levinas writes: 'Accusing oneself in suffering is undoubtedly the very turning back of the *I* to itself. It is perhaps thus that the for-the-other – the most upright relation to the other – is the most profound adventure of subjectivity, its ultimate intimacy. But this intimacy can only be discreetly. It cannot give itself out as an example, or be narrated in an edifying discourse. It cannot, without being perverted, be made into a preachment' (p. 99).

14. To the extent that Job is a critical reference point for Levinas in thinking opposition to theodicy, it is not simply the case that the refusal of theodicy entails a departure from Biblical traditions. Levinas contemplates Philippe Nemo's 'book about evil in Job' in his essay 'Transcendence and Evil'.

15. Levinas's thinking may be contrasted to that found in Elaine Scarry's influential 1980s book, *The Body in Pain: The Making and Unmaking of the World* (New York and Oxford: Oxford University Press, 1985), which is also relevant for the present study. Levinas's thinking of the suffering of the other does not entail simply a reversal of the analysis found in *The Body in Pain* (influenced, as the latter is, more by the analytic tradition rather than the continental). This is in the sense that it does not operate in terms of, and therefore merely subvert, the same conceptual field. Nevertheless, there is a striking contrast between the two. For Scarry, while the pain of the other is always susceptible to doubt, denial or disregard, one's own pain is undeniably certain. For Levinas, on the contrary, while one's own pain can never be fully available as such, experienced without remainder by the consciousness it is in fact 'in-spite-of', the 'call for aid' entailed by the other's suffering is radically undeniable in the sense that it irremissibly *demands*. This is the case, even though Levinas in *Time and the Other* (Pittsburgh: Duquesne University Press, 1987) writes: 'While in moral pain one can preserve an attitude of dignity and compunction, and consequently already be free; physical suffering in all its degrees entails the impossibility of detaching oneself from the instant of existence. It is the very irremissibility of being. The content of suffering merges with the impossibility of detaching oneself from suffering . . . In suffering there is an absence of all refuge . . . The whole actuality of suffering lies in this impossibility of retreat.' However, crucially, he goes on: 'But in suffering there is, at the same time . . . the proximity of death . . . pain of itself includes it like a paroxysm, as if there were something about to be produced even more rending than suffering, as if despite the entire absence of a dimension of withdrawal that constitutes suffering, it still had some free space for an event, as if it must still get uneasy about something, as if we were on the verge of an event beyond what is revealed to the end in suffering. The structure of pain, which consists in its very attachment to pain, is prolonged further, but up to an unknown that is impossible to translate in terms of light – that is, that is refractory to the intimacy of the self with the ego to which all our experiences return' (p. 69). While my own pain – although impossible to discount – nonetheless leaves me, in its very inescapability, at the impossible threshold of an event to come, it is the other's pain that foremost claims me, indeed claims my own. It does so, in a similar way that the death of the

other as 'first death' constitutes itself, as Derrida in *The Gift of Death* points out, as a death for which I am responsible, up to the point of including myself in this death. This death of the other as 'first death', of course, puts in question the Heideggerian notion of death as Dasein's most proper or own-most possibility (i.e. one's own death as the foremost of being). But it also leads to the proposition that I am responsible for the other inasmuch as he is mortal. That is to say, the basic structure of Levinasian responsibility pertains to the question of suffering in a similar way to that of death: it is not a case of 'I think', 'I suffer', 'I die', 'therefore I am'. Instead, like death, suffering – to the extent that it can mean anything at all, or, better still, be 'suffered' at all – comes from the other.

16. See Levinas, *Difficult Freedom: Essays on Judaism*, trans. Seán Hand (London: Athlone, 1990), p. 49.
17. Graeber for one seems keen to dispute this 'origin story'.

Chapter 1

After Pains

Nachkriege: Ernst Jünger's 'On Pain'

In the period after the First World War, the sense of extreme national humiliation that resulted in a historical experience of *Nachkriege* or 'afterwar' on the part of the German Right, in particular, took the form not only of a mortifying sense of loss but, perhaps as its further radicalisation, a refusal to accept the war's ending. ('Afterwar', then, can be read in a double and contradictory sense.) As we shall see, in 'Theories of German Fascism', which reviewed the work of Ernst Jünger, Walter Benjamin argues that this tendency to continually relive the last war, to permanently inhabit its milieu, not only prevented Germany from accepting and capitalising on loss (as Benjamin believed had happened in Russia). Through a particular aestheticisation of politics, the deep repressions characterising this climate of 'lost war' also funded a disastrous misconstrual of the stakes and conditions of the next one. It is in this context of *Nachkriege*, then, that the rise of an ultra-conservative reactionary modernism[1] can be understood, as the broader yet somewhat distinct backdrop for the specifically Hitlerian form that German fascism took. Such reactionary modernism mobilised itself, as Peter Osborne has observed, on the strength of a specific temporal structure defined by the 'conjunction of a backward-looking politics', on the one hand (in Jünger's case, a politics based on the vision of a soldierly heroism wholly at odds with the values of progressive liberalism, representative government, individual freedom, security, convenience and comfort that he saw as responsible for the crisis of European modernity), and, on the other, 'an affirmation of technology' that was futurally oriented, and indeed imbued with a warlike destiny.[2] Of the different forms this reactionary modernism took, during the 1920s and early 1930s Jünger developed an ultra-austere vision of an anti-democratic worker-state based on soldierly discipline, order and sacrifice. At the heart of this was placed the transformative capacity of modern technology, closely allied to a cult of war which desired total and permanent mobilisation as the basis of a radically new social form. As Osborne notes, such reactionary politics were therefore not only opposed to modernity but constituted precisely a form of modernism, in that they sought not so much to conserve or defend an already lost past as to create the conditions for the full realisation of this past '*for the first time*' – inventing its possibility anew, stripped of all the perceived imperfections or constraints that led to the demise of such a 'past' in the first place (p. 164). For Osborne, this recognition of the 'modernistic temporality of reaction' is important in understanding more broadly the highly complicated, radically unstable and yet massively extended 'upsurge of revolutionary ideologies of both "reactionary" and "progressive" types' in the aftermath of the crisis of nineteenth-century European ideological and social forms. However, given that – notwithstanding its futural orientation – such reactionary modernism makes its case on the strength of a backward-looking affirmation of prized elements of the past, Osborne identifies the key contradiction internal to and constitutive of its own make-up, 'since one of the things it aims to reverse is the production of the very temporality to which it is itself subject' (p. 167). Reactionary modernism must therefore embrace or 'performatively affirm' what it seeks to overcome, and yet somehow supersede that to which it must also give itself: modernity itself.

The name that Jünger albeit unwittingly gives this experience of contradiction is, one might venture, pain. I will attempt to show why this may be so. If nineteenth-century values had eroded all absolute standards or 'binding norms', for Jünger the experience of physical pain constituted an elementary and ineluctable threshold that shed light nonetheless upon the historical conditions of 'man's stature' at any one time.[3] Or, as Jünger himself puts it: 'Pain as a measure of man is unalterable, but what can be altered is the way he confronts it' (p. 1). Pain, in other words, is 'the true testing ground of reality' (p. 45); more ominously, 'the movement toward pain endures as an astonishing sign of the times' (constituting as it does, albeit rather grandiosely, the 'negative mark of a metaphysical structure' that comes to the fore in this 'last and indeed quite remarkable phase of nihilism' (pp. 46–7)). For Jünger, then, such an affirmation of pain opposes the sickliness of nineteenth-century culture, remedying the 'deadly cultural diseases' of European civilisation. Not least, this affirmation combats the desire for 'shelter', 'safety' or 'security' which drives 'technical and political conveniences' like the abolition of torture and slavery, the development of vaccines and systems of insurance, and so on – all of which dim the adventurous, noble spirit that connects Jünger to a certain Nietzschean inheritance (pp. 9–10). Pain jolts the 'complacency' and 'predictability' of effete social and political forms (p. 11). It strikes a blow at trivial 'ease', empty 'freedom' and self-gratifying pleasure (p. 12). If, indeed, 'the fabulous expansion of technical means' has undeniably aided 'pure convenience' (p. 13), nonetheless to the extent that technology makes possible an 'assault that is colder and more rapacious than any other' (p. 4), it also creates the opportunity for a yet more exceptional affirmation of pain. (For Jünger, photography as much as military technology – of which it nevertheless forms a part – participates in just such an 'assault', and its 'peculiarly cruel way of seeing' is therefore to be considered a weapon in the service of the wholly estranging reactionary future he imagines (pp. 38–40).) Furthermore, the easing of pain, for Jünger, amounts to little more than its repression,[4] leading as it does to the crippling 'boredom' that is 'nothing other than the dissolution of pain in time' (p. 13). Such boredom is further described by Jünger in terms of a slavish 'embitterment' that constitutes an inferior and unhealthy form of pain, one that gives rise to the sickly science of psychology. (Jünger goes on to contrast psychological self-reflection upon the 'sensitive' human being with a colder 'second consciousness' devoted to a heroically accomplished relation to pain achieved through the objectification of the body (p. 38).) Indeed, the desire to extract pain from time, to restore it to its proper condition or state (namely the instantaneous experience of physical violence in war), connects to an anxiety or ambivalence about pain that Jünger himself seeks to repress, one that links in turn to the temporal structure of reactionary modernism that Osborne describes. For if pain of the Jüngerian type is pitched against 'sensitivity' in all its (cultural) forms, then the question arises as to whether the truly heroic attitude relates to an intensified experience of pain or, just the opposite, its total overcoming. For all its manly frisson, wouldn't indulging in pain come perilously close to the sublime 'sensitivity' so prevalent in, let's say, post-Romantic bourgeois culture, or wouldn't it at any rate share some of its structural conditions? For sure, Jünger foresees this objection, but handles it rather uncertainly. He alludes to a certain treatment of the body as object by means of which pain is not to be avoided, but mastered. Indeed, pain is to be cultivated and controlled or commanded by way of a 'heroic worldview' that cannot be artificially contrived but which must be authentically inherited. Thus writes Jünger:

> The heroic and cultic world presents an entirely different relation to pain than does the world of sensitivity. While in the latter, as we saw, it is a matter of marginalizing pain and sheltering life from it, in the former the point is

to integrate pain and organize life in such a way that one is always armed against it. (p. 16)

Students of the post-Romantic bourgeois culture to which I just now alluded (albeit with reductive haste) will no doubt question whether, throughout the texts and artefacts of this culture, anything ever boils down simply to a matter of 'marginalizing pain and sheltering life from it'. (The question of sublimity, to which the present book devotes many pages, alone testifies to this.) Even if one wishes to stay with Jünger's term, the 'sensitive' relation to pain is surely more complex and contradictory than that, as Freud and a host of others have taught us. It is telling, then, that Jünger is so quick to set up a non-complex opposition between sensitivity and heroism, in which the unproblematised image of the former in effect upholds and reflects the presumed consistency and integrity of the latter. And what threatens to disrupt such presumed consistency and integrity is the question of whether, by integrating or mastering pain, one opens oneself to it all the more profoundly, or arms oneself against it all the more effectively. Which is the more heroic gesture? To avoid 'sensitive' indulgence, one must tirelessly resist the very same pain with which one must nevertheless remain in ceaseless contact in order to live life in its heroic form.[5] And yet, whether or not in different shape or guise, that (obsessive) resistance to/of pain is also surely a feature of bourgeois civilisation (and its doubleness the very mark of the sublime)? Put another way, a straightforward contrast and opposition between heroism and sensitivity falters at the point both expose themselves to pain *in the very form of a certain resistance to it*. This ambivalent relation to pain when conceived of as *a repressed ambivalence toward the other* translates the double desire to admit and resist the other, to at once acknowledge and reject the other. To embrace what it seeks to overcome and yet somehow to supersede that to which it must also give itself: this was our definition, earlier, of reactionary modernism's relation to modernity itself. The connection between pain and modernistic temporality might not amount to just an empty analogy. Jünger's desire to extract pain from time, i.e. to affirm pain in the form of an instantaneous (warlike) experience of physical violence, is also evidence of the pain *of* time construed – on the basis of Jünger's own contradictory discourse – as just such an ambivalent relation to the other. Indeed, Jünger's allusion to the objectification of the body as a means to transcend merely physical pain in a more truly heroic fashion itself militates against the image of pain as just materially present or corporeally immediate, as if Jünger wants to trace a more heroic attitude to pain within and against this bodily experience, thus – in the very process of delineation – dividing anew its supposed purity or integrity. Hence he writes later in the text that it is to be considered 'a mark of superior achievement when life gains distance from itself, or, in other words, when it is able to sacrifice itself', presumably by withstanding the pain to which it is subjected to the point of death – again, an image of at once total resistance and total exposure to pain (p. 31). Pain's true purity, in other words, is concocted from an admixture of apparent opposites or contrasting elements that vie somewhat uneasily, or painfully, with one another: contact and distance, endurance and resistance of pain, physical experience and its overcoming, immediacy and transcendence, inheritance and futurity, and so on. Just as the heroic stance distinguishes itself precisely in relation to the 'zone of pain' from which it takes a certain distance, so the 'sensitive' relationship to pain is distinguished, in what turns out to be an uncanny rather than fully confrontational relation, as much by a (weakly) succumbing to pain, as by a (cowardly) sheltering from it. Relatedly, too (and not unlike technology itself), the narcotics that shield us from pain also enhance the conditions under which the body can be treated 'objectively', as Jünger himself acknowledges (p. 44), so that the interaction between the culture of sensitivity and the onset of heroism as a 'cultic entity' (p. 46) is not simply reducible to frontal opposition.

In view of such complex interactions, going beyond straightforward polarities, it is important to recall that, just as for Osborne modernistic temporality gave rise to revolutionary forms of both reactionary and progressive sorts, so the double appeal to pain's endurance and resistance on Jünger's part finds its not-too-distant echo in the notion of the resistant subject as 'already dead'. As Howard Caygill has put it, speaking of the Zapatistas in particular, 'the living resistants should live as if already dead': the resistant subject 'is not free to choose a life of resistance, but is already dead and so must resist.'[6] Constituted by conditions of oppression over which they have no living choice, the Zapatistas as resistant subjects nevertheless become dead to the living death that such oppression asks them to endure. They live on only in respect of the 'universality of the call to resistance' that derives from all those who will have lived and died in oppression's clutches (in other words, they belong to the dead). Such resistant subjects are therefore characterised not just by a certain preparedness to die, but by the dead form in which they properly exist. Such subjects, not unlike Jünger's warrior-workers, are to be recognised principally in terms of the sacrifice which exposes them to the possibility of the most radical endurance of pain – an experience to which, as the 'already dead', they are nonetheless in a certain way wholly inured.

While the Zapatistas are Caygill's preferred example in this regard, Martin McQuillan has recently discussed the upsurge within contemporary theoretical writing of what he terms a Maoist political theology that introduces a newly violent tone (as McQuillan himself puts it) into the field of continental philosophy,[7] focusing his remarks on Žižek's introduction to Robespierre's defence of revolutionary terror.[8] Several passages from Žižek's essay are painstakingly analysed by McQuillan in order to produce a powerful critique of such a logic as is developed here. One in particular stands out for our purposes (I refer to the original text in which this appears). Žižek writes:

> In short, how can Robespierre be sure that the process he has unleashed will not swallow him up? It is here that his position takes on a sublime greatness – he fully assumes the danger that now threatens Danton will tomorrow threaten him. The reason that he is so serene, that he is not afraid of this fate, is not that Danton was a traitor, while he, Robespierre, is pure, a direct embodiment of the people's Will; it is that he, Robespierre, is not afraid to die – his eventual death will be a mere accident which counts for nothing: 'What does danger matter to me? My life belongs to the homeland; my heart is free from fear; and if I were to die, I would do so without reproach and without ignominy.' Consequently, insofar as the shift from 'we' to 'I' can effectively be determined as the moment when the democratic mask falls down and when Robespierre openly asserts himself as a Master . . . the term Master has to be given here its full Hegelian weight: the Master is the figure of sovereignty, the one who is not afraid to die, who is ready to risk everything. In other words, the ultimate meaning of Robespierre's first-person singular ('I') is: I am not afraid to die. (p. xvii)

Citing the Zen priest Yamamoto Jocho, Žižek suggests that the genuinely revolutionary stance is not to live for political emancipation but instead 'to consider oneself dead beforehand' (p. xvii). (We will let go the reference to the sublime in the above passage from Žižek, and, as we'll see, its recursion below, although it should perhaps be noted in terms of the complexities addressed, above, in our discussion of Jünger.) As McQuillan observes, at this point Žižek alludes to those Japanese soldiers during the Second World War who conducted their own funerals before going to fight, noting here the inter-implication of the position of the revolutionary with that of the warrior, one that is redolent of Jünger in many respects. (Of course, as McQuillan is all too aware, Žižek's discourse also unavoidably gestures towards the suicide bombers of today, the French term for which is 'kamikaze'; interestingly, Jünger's 'On Pain' begins with a Japanese epigraph that alludes to harakiri.) Žižek goes on: 'This pre-emptive self-exclusion from the domain of the living of course turns the soldier into a properly sublime figure. Instead of dismissing this feature as part of Fascist militarism, one should assert it as also constitutive of a radical revolutionary position' (p. xviii). At this, McQuillan snorts in derision: 'Sorry, there was me mistaking theocratic death cults with Fascist militarism, how bourgeois of me' (p. 178). Now, I don't want to rehearse further McQuillan's powerfully polemical critique of this text, nor do I aim either to extend or criticise it here, except to note that in this moment of the essay it is, paradoxically, he, rather than Žižek, who endeavours more firmly to split off fascism as a somewhat more discrete entity.[9] Hence I do think it is important to underscore, on the basis of the discussion we've developed so far, that in terms of its conditions of possibility at least, 'fascist militarism' cannot be so hastily set aside – by the revolutionary or anybody else – if one wishes to think about the 'upsurge of revolutionary ideologies of both "reactionary" and "progressive" types' that in turn recalls modernity's sense of crisis (something which we may still experience, perhaps, in the form taken by *Nachkriege*).

Living Lost War: Jünger, Benjamin and Strauss

Perhaps one of the best-known responses to Jünger's post-First World War political writings is that of Walter Benjamin, who in 1930 published his review of a collection of essays, *Krieg und Krieger*, edited by Jünger. 'Theories of German Fascism' was to be the title under which Benjamin addressed this volume.[10] (In helping to lay the ground for Benjamin's famous argument about the aestheticisation of politics, this text is often considered to be the dialectical partner of his review of Erich Kastner's poetry, 'Left-Wing Melancholy', published in 1931.[11]) Benjamin begins his text by acknowledging the question of an unreconciled relationship of technology to society, not just in the postwar context but in view of the very problem of war as itself far from resolved and, in this sense, still imminent. Nonetheless, he is quick to repudiate the mystification of war as a generalised phenomenon or universalisable experience susceptible to the aesthetic and political intentions of a reactionary modernism. Paradoxically, Benjamin points out, such an essentialist view of war in fact adopts a central principle of pacifism (i.e. the reduction or levelling of all wars to a conception of war as such). Nonetheless, for Benjamin 'Jünger's mysticism of war' (p. 121), being a throwback to prewar conceptions of soldierly heroism as much as a fearful phenomenon of the postwar period, remains even less well equipped than all-out pacifism to comprehend the conditions of possibility of 'the next war'. (For Benjamin, this 'next war' will be much less the 'incisive magical turning point' of nationalist myth than the simple reflection of 'everyday actuality' in need of materialist analysis as such (p. 128).) Interestingly, some of the key observations that inform Benjamin's critique of this reactionary mysticism of war – concerning not just the technological transformation of the means of war but also, for instance, the displacement of 'soldierly qualities' into those of the modern sportsman – are incorporated into the theoretical fabric of 'On Pain', which appeared just four years later. In Jünger's essay, the stripping away of the personal or individualistic qualities of the combatant (or, for that matter, civilian) due to the impossibility of defence against the new machinic instruments of mass warfare is not taken to signal the end of heroism. Instead, such depersonalisation in fact facilitates the advent of the soldier-worker, hardened by and to suffering, who is thereafter valiantly equipped to confront the ruins of prewar bourgeois culture. As such, the erosion of any distinction between the civilian population and military personnel that Benjamin considers a profound threat to the basis of international law (and thereby the regulation of warfare) is viewed by Jünger as the potential ground of a total militarisation that would not only have changed the negative outcome of the last war, but that establishes the heroic possibility of a revolutionary ultra-conservatism. Far from being repudiated, the prospect of total or 'endless' war foreseen by Benjamin in 1930 is thus embraced wholeheartedly by Jünger.

Be that as it may, Benjamin rejects the possibility that a cult of war can truly survive modern technologies of warfare or, more particularly, that heroic conceptions of military endeavour can have any authentic future in post-First World War Germany itself. Indeed, the irony of Jüngerian politics from a Benjaminian point of view is that by truculently strengthening its ensemble of ideas, it further weakens its position or argument, intensifying its standpoint as merely a form of denial, a misguided reaction to its own repressed actuality (although no less dangerous for all that). For if the clarion call of war for war's sake – 'an uninhibited translation of the principles of *l'art pour l'art*' (p. 122) – would seem to facilitate some terrible identity between the nihilism of the machine and the cult of total violence, it nonetheless fails to come to terms with the fact that, 'in the controversy over the war, which has convulsed Germany since 1919', what is 'characteristically German' is the indisputable sense of defeat, which is really at the basis of cultic belligerence (p. 123). Thus the rise of ultra-conservative reaction represents a desperate response to the irrefutable *loss* of war as much as it testifies to the possibility of war's total extension as such. As Benjamin puts it, the loser must live *without* the war, whereas those of Jünger's ilk are capable only of fantasising eternal combat (in the process, losing sight of the fact that it is only the winner who enjoys the luxury of keeping the war 'in hand', in Benjamin's terms). Incapable of 'holding up to view', and instead just 'doggedly holding onto', that which had been lost, in Benjamin's eyes Jünger represents a Germany incapable of capitalising on loss, as other nations had done. (In this regard, Benjamin alludes to Russia's great success in the interwar period.) As the old saying goes, you don't win the next war by fighting the last one – much less by evoking the qualities of war as 'eternal and primeval', in a way that relies merely on the 'journalistic haste to capitalize from the actual present without grasping the past' (p. 122). Knowing nothing of peace, men like Jünger make claims to war that remain as empty as those of 'professional freebooters' (p. 126). Meanwhile, Benjamin laments the pervasive potential of 'humbug about . . . arch-Germanic fate' which, even when countered by 'a truly dialectic spirit' such as his close friend Florens Christian Rang, can nevertheless re-emerge, in Rang's case in the form of laments about past military shortcomings, taking the form of a perceived deficit of bravery. (In the latter, indeed, we find a dim echo of the demand for total mobilisation, since this demand draws much of its force from an insistence upon the cowardliness of partial mobilisation during the First World War). For Benjamin, then, such attitudes, whether fuelled by pugnacious self-assurance or mournful retrospection, permeate the German sense of defeat, inhibiting materialist analysis through the intensifying aestheticisation of politics. Technology is not, however, fated to join forces with a death-bound heroism. This is evident not just from Benjamin's own conception of technological possibility, whereby, as he puts it, the disaster of the next war might be averted if human relationships were to be ordered in accord with the relationship to nature made possible by technology (p. 128). For Benjamin, it is also apparent in the fact that some of those contributing to Jünger's collection of essays cannot help but betray their disappointment in the technological form of war, or, by repressing this sense of disappointment, are forced to embrace, as Benjamin puts it, the 'dependable fascist class warrior' (p. 127) in a way that utterly distorts the conservative penchant for soldierly nobility. Modern ultra-reactionary myth, not technology, mobilises the fascist state form in relationship to a conception of war that is not so much destined as disastrously determined in 'mystical' ways. As Benjamin astutely observes, the militarised hordes serve the purposes not merely of a fascist ideal, but perhaps more significantly they benefit the interests of those 'captains of finance' and 'masters of inflation' for whom the pre-fascist state was 'beginning to seem a dubious guarantor of their property' (p. 127). Thus Jünger's worker-soldiers do not simply give up their individual subjectivities or personal identities in the service of a high-minded ideal. Instead, whether knowingly or not, they exist only to be bought and sold amid a distinctively postwar economy of interests. The capacities of such men (for instance, the pilot of a single airplane loaded with gas bombs in whom is concentrated the absolute power over 'a citizen's light, air and life' that was previously distributed 'among thousands of office managers' (p. 128)) do not draw their force from the ideal of an ultra-reactionary nationalist heroism so much as from the particular configuration of the state in its modern form (including its relationship to private interests), a form which Benjamin sees as at once dangerously powerful and 'seriously stricken' – at any rate, a state in the process of transition that the politics of men like Jünger can only capitalise upon opportunistically, rather than lead or determine in more authentic terms.

Obviously, the intention of Benjamin's critique is to demythologise and hence delegitimise ultra-reactionary politics of the Jüngerian stripe by pointing up their fundamental contradictions and repressions. Thus he concludes his text by asserting that, in the sense that such contradictions are evidence of the crisis of postwar culture, they must be forcibly exposed and overcome by performing that 'Marxist trick' of converting the warlike atmosphere of ultra-reactionary conservatism into the conditions for a socially transformative 'civil war'. This 'war' alone would be capable of capitalising on the loss of 'war' that Jünger's writing both eschews and laments (p. 128).

A decade later, reference to Jünger's 'On Pain' is put to a different use, by a thinker whose political outlook and influence is strikingly different, although no less complicated, than Benjamin's.[12] In 1940, Leo Strauss wrote a lecture on 'The Living Issues of German Postwar Philosophy', presented to the Creighton Philosophical Club on the occasion of its thirty-ninth meeting at Syracuse University, one that was to go unpublished until long after his death.[13] The allusion to Jünger is admittedly brief and does not occur until well into the second half of the text, but is nevertheless significant in the sense that 'On Pain' is taken as the 'more radical expression' of a longing and quest for authority that, for Strauss, had come to preoccupy certain German philosophers over recent decades.[14] Strauss wants to offer a rather involved philosophical interpretation of this longing. It is therefore necessary to track back through the lecture in order to understand the importance of Strauss's mention of Jünger in terms of a wider explanation on Strauss's part of the meaning of the German psyche after the First World War, one that contrasts strongly with that of Benjamin.

For Strauss, civilisation in Germany is less mature than in other European nations and yet is characterised by a more critical attitude to the very idea of civilisation, especially in its modern version. (Strauss observes that such criticality, so vital in the realm of philosophy, is nonetheless 'disastrous' when transposed into the political field.) If civilisation itself marks a certain turning away from nature, or a particular neglect in relation to one's natural condition, for Strauss it is the basic task of philosophy to acquire a 'living knowledge' (p. 115) of this same circumstance, which in turn necessarily places philosophy at one remove from civilisation (not its 'outside' exactly, but nevertheless the complex site of a certain non-coincidence).

Strauss observes that the German dissatisfaction with modern civilisation constitutes itself in terms of a yearning for the past, which in its cruder manifestation prizes the Teutonic inheritance, but which in its more enlightened form seeks knowledge and experience of classical antiquity. Here, Strauss alludes to the well-known attempts within German philosophy to discern deep connections between the Greek philosophical past and the historical spirit and destiny of Germany, notably in terms of the Nietzschean and subsequently Heideggerian desire to take classical forms of thought as the wellspring for the critique of modernity. For Strauss, this criticism of modern civilisation concentrates on one of its most prominent features, modern science. Hence, Hegelian thought is characterised by its concern to distinguish history as a realm of freedom in opposition to nature as a realm of necessity (whether it be mechanical or mathematical necessity). Similarly, says Strauss, in contrast to rational construction Hegel asserts dialectical process. However, in terms of postwar German philosophy the principal tension for Strauss is not that of history versus nature or organic versus scientific development, but it is instead 'life or existence vs. science, science being *any* purely theoretical enterprise' (p. 116). Thus, both natural and historical science fall within the purview of this critique.

Strauss identifies two types of postwar German philosophy, going beyond the work of purely 'academic philosophers' (p. 117) who sought to maintain some continuity with the prewar past. First of all, he notes the 'superficial' trend of certain eye-catching forms of philosophical thought that exerted a more 'direct', 'revolutionizing' influence on the impressionable sectors of 'academic youth'. Beneath this, Strauss detects the more modest yet profound attitude of those thinkers struggling to re-establish philosophical enquiry with regard to the 'nature of things' (p. 117), along the lines of his earlier evocation of philosophy's principal task. Strauss decides to concentrate on the former grouping only insofar as their interests are in fact symptomatic of, and therefore shed light upon, a deeper set of concerns that lead us towards the endeavours of the latter.

Strauss notes Spengler's pugnacious attack on modern science and philosophy as embodying in themselves merely the expression of specific cultural values, which for Strauss leaves philosophy and science in the position of relativism, contrasting this with Max Weber's defence of modern scientific and philosophical enquiry. Spengler's teaching, then, elaborates a philosophy of man as essentially a historical being (Strauss here places Heidegger in this tradition). Philosophy conceived of as an essentially historical practice is thereby reduced to hermeneutical activity. And yet to properly grasp the texts, cultures and artefacts of the past in their true meanings, one must dispense with or work beyond the categories and concepts of the present, of which cultural relativism would be one (indeed, hermeneutics would be another). The dilemma here, then, would seem to be that in order for it to be possible, such historico-philosophical endeavour must forego that which makes it possible. If philosophical historicism finds itself in an aporia of its own making, nevertheless a more elemental philosophy – which by returning to pre-scientific or pre-philosophical language and thought is, for Strauss, not merely reduced to the historicist dilemma – still begs the question of (its own) authority. (As we shall see, Strauss continues to locate this authority in the 'natural' task of philosophy, albeit that this 'nature' is complexly evoked.) If, in other words, 'radical historicism awakens a passionate interest in the past and therewith a passionate interest in the unhistorical approach characteristic of man up to the 18th century', Strauss must address the question of what necessitates and indeed authorises the resurgence of this 'unhistorical' approach outside of or beyond modern historicism itself (notwithstanding that the latter teeters on the edge of its own legitimation crisis).

If the tendency in postwar German philosophy that Strauss alludes to by way of Spengler amounts to the pursuit of 'self-knowledge of man in his historicity' (p. 121), for Strauss this nevertheless comes down to a purely theoretical practice of both history and philosophy to which, he reminds us, Nietzsche would have objected. Historical knowledge, as the form human self-knowledge takes, constitutes itself according to a process of reflection which threatens to dim spontaneity, lived life, or living historical possibility. History cannot be made out of historical studies alone. History itself is the proof of this, not least since most of history happened prior to the historical consciousness that emerged in philosophical form in the eighteenth century. For similar reasons, one might think that historical studies could not answer the question of its own motivation without going outside of or beyond its own practice, or in other words without addressing the question of 'why and how far historical consciousness is a necessity'

(p. 122), which it would presumably find difficult to confront alone (i.e. 'historicistically'), without support from elsewhere. Nevertheless, Strauss tells us, to the extent that the question of its 'necessity' may be deemed a historical one, we must go beyond Nietzsche in order to explore the historical reasons for the modern advent of historical studies as a form of 'necessity'. (Strauss takes this approach, I think, to ensure that his own philosophical preferences are protected as much as possible from the looming crisis of authority: in other words, the 'necessity' of historical consciousness is precisely that it makes – historically – necessary other forms of philosophy oriented toward classical antiquity or the authority of 'nature', which can be rendered distinct from the unthinking authoritarianism upon which fascists and other reactionary or totalitarian forces rely.)

In order to have his historical cake and eat it, or in other words to move both within and outside of historicist authority, Strauss makes the following arguments. First, he suggests that human life is essentially historical. It is so in the sense that it is always lived according to tradition, and by way of traditional ensembles of ideas, concepts and practices (even if that tradition is one of anti-traditionalism – for instance, post-Descartes – and thus, for Strauss, somewhat blind to its own traditions, just as historicism remains blind to its own historical conditions and limits). But, paradoxically, this affirmation once more necessitates a movement or gesture that goes beyond the limits of the current historicist mindset. Historical studies are not so much the apogee of modern civilisation or thought, the serene completion of all historical practice; rather, they are 'necessary because of the *bankruptcy* of modern man', and as such they define him in his need to escape himself (p. 125). Put another way, 'the most important motive for historical studies' is 'a turning to the thought of the past' that might itself offer some passage beyond the constraining dilemma of historicism itself.

Yet this passage toward a remote and forgotten past cannot be expressed as anything less than a search for (non-relative) truth, a quest for significance rather than merely (scientific) progress, regardless of the fact that historicism registers the fulfilment of such a task as impossible. (Later in the essay, Strauss argues that the 'liberation' of philosophy from historicism is not its 'refutation'; it constitutes not a return to pre-historicist dogmatism so much as a flight from dogma, of which historicism can prove to be one kind, towards a fresh approach to the – historical – problem of the 'historical' (p. 133).) Such a desire, argues Strauss, was experienced in Germany by 'the thinking part of the academic youth' after the turmoil of the First World War had placed in severe jeopardy prewar values of all sorts. In this context, Max Weber's defence of modern science and philosophy as forms of knowledge that draw their limit at the question of meaning proved at once problematic and illuminating. As Strauss puts it, Weber argues that 'reason and argument are intrinsically incapable of giving to life a real guidance' (p. 127), so that any decisions we make on this front (i.e. with regard to life's meaning, significance or value) are essentially 'irrational'. Indeed, for this same reason, even outright opposition to the scientific approach cannot be legitimately refuted by science itself, since such opposition amounts to a value-based or 'life' choice over which science can have no valid say. But the problem then becomes this. If human life is indeed oriented by tradition, as Strauss suggests, which tradition might now orient postwar life in terms of the realms opened up by historical studies through which, nonetheless, historical studies cannot properly lead us? Strauss's answer is that if in Germany 'traditions were losing their force more and more . . . people had no choice but to turn away from reason to authority' (p. 127). What we are left with is, on the one hand, cruder forms of thinking which convert historical consciousness or tradition into what Benjamin called 'humbug about . . . arch-Germanic fate' in order to submit to authority without question and, on the other, elementary philosophical possibility of the kind Strauss detects as the more profound (if much less visible and more widely suppressed) reaction to the postwar condition.

'The most visible kind of authority – most visible at least in Germany – is the State' (p. 127): Strauss makes this remark in order to direct us towards the work of Carl Schmitt and to introduce his particular 'chain of thought'. Since no set of values or ideals can enjoy rational supremacy, they are a matter of personal preference and individual decision in the private sphere. For this same reason, no one man can with any validity elevate his ideals above those of another. Yet at the same time no political community can exist without extracting obligations from its members, obligations that necessarily overrule private freedoms. While in terms of its values the political community enjoys no more and no less legitimacy than the individual characterised by his personal choices, it nevertheless imposes obligations that must be absolute (i.e. 'the obligation to sacrifice life itself' (p. 127)), precisely in the sense that were they just 'conditional obligations' they would lead back toward merely individual or personal values and preferences. Put another way, it is precisely because these obligations are not conditional that the authority of the state is not rational. And since it could never be rational, what in Schmittian terms authorises the state is the friend-enemy distinction that pertains in reference to the permanent possibility of war. As Strauss puts it:

> The basic fact of the possibility of war sets an absolute limit to all freedom of decision: it creates *authority* and therewith it gives all members of the community a generally valid guidance. (p. 128)

This boils down to the paradox that in its state-form authority not only begs its own question but exists as an answer on precisely this same basis. In other words, a certain deficit of authority that defines authority as such does not simply threaten to weaken the state's claims and demands, since such a deficit makes it possible and indeed necessary as a form of authority in the first place. (This paradox also connects to the problem of political theology that is an abiding interest of Strauss's; here, it is described in terms of science, philosophy or culture proving unable to adequately serve the interests of humankind without the supplement of divine or political authority.)

It is at this point in the lecture that Jünger's essay crops up as the 'more radical expression of this view' hitherto associated with Schmitt (p. 128). The drastic decline of past values and traditions, which have now lost both 'their force and evidence', combined with the Schmittian sense of individual decisions as merely 'conditional', leaves us in a situation whereby, for Jünger, 'there is one standard left', a stand-alone virtue which might be held in common, namely 'the ability or inability to stand pain, physical pain'. Thus, to follow the Schmittian 'chain of thought' once more, the state would on this Jüngerian view need to be based on the simple standard of 'fortitude or courage', without prior reason or purpose, rather than upon any form of mutual rationality, collective decision or even shared interest as such. (One might observe that this makes the state-form as precarious as it is strong, something to which Jünger would far from wholly object in the sense that for him strength is based on the permanent possibility of all-out war.)

If, then, Benjamin sees Jünger as a symptom of the repression of loss brought on by the war, whose defining contradictions might nevertheless be transformed into the conditions for radical social change, Strauss explains Jünger's emergence and relative prominence in terms of a crisis of historical consciousness bequeathed to us by the Enlightenment. If, for both, the phenomenon of Jünger's work suggests a certain crisis or terminal point in the history of European civilisation, for Benjamin its arrival points us towards an alternative future (already embedded in the conditions of the present) that we can only grasp by dint of a certain 'Marxist trick', whereas for Strauss it drives us backwards to the hoped-for experience of classical antiquity which might be capable of redeeming philosophy's elementary or 'natural' task and with it, perhaps, the very plight of historical civilisation. (Here, between Benjamin and

Strauss, we seem once again to be in the midst of modernity's double-time.) Both obviously reject – or, rather, reinterpret – Jünger's specific interpretation of postwar 'pain', albeit according to very different motivations. Nevertheless, to borrow Deleuze's terms, both see Jünger as something of a symptom ('the specific sign of an illness') for which a syndrome ('the meeting-place or crossing point of manifestations issuing from very different origins') must be diagnosed and indeed subjected to discriminating analysis.[15] That is to say, while neither accept 'pain' on Jünger's own terms, both acknowledge – albeit in strikingly different ways – that Jünger's thought on the topic is itself pained, the product of a certain malady or ailment that needs treatment or intervention in some sense. And, in either case, such treatment will inevitably be painful, difficult, fraught in one way or another. For Strauss, a return to 'natural' rather than abstract or derivative (historicist) philosophy involves – indeed, draws its authority from – the full historicisation of the historicism that in other ways blights us. Such a task is not yet entirely within the scope of our imagination. For Benjamin, meanwhile, social transformation becomes possible on the strength of another experience of loss than that shrouded in denial. Neither of these pathways looks painless, in other words – as if coming to terms with a modern cult of pain as itself the perceived symptom of world-historical crisis could only be accessed by recourse to pain of some other kind.[16]

Notes

1. This term is taken from the title of Jeffrey Herf's *Reactionary Modernism: Technology, Culture, and Politics in Weimar and the Third Reich* (Cambridge: Cambridge University Press, 1984), which needless to say analyses the phenomenon of 'reactionary modernism' in great detail. Herf's book is given an interesting critical treatment by Peter Osborne in *The Politics of Time: Modernity and Avant-Garde* (London and New York: Verso, 1995), the arguments of which this chapter goes on to discuss.
2. See Peter Osborne, *The Politics of Time*, p. 163.
3. Ernst Jünger, *On Pain*, trans. David C. Durst (New York: Telos Press, 2008), pp. 1–2. All further page references will be given in the main body of the chapter.
4. Jünger writes of 'the sum of pain that remains unclaimed and amasses as hidden capital accruing compound interest' (p. 15). Later, he remarks that pain 'demands payback on its outstanding debt' (p. 27). On the strength of the analysis I am seeking to develop here, it would no doubt be interesting to analyse the relationship of *Nachkriege* and indeed the very time of modernism to the emergence of debt capitalism. As we shall see further along in the present chapter, Benjamin links the rise of German fascism to the economic interests of 'captains of finance' and 'masters of inflation'. In the

chapter on debt in the present book, meanwhile, I want to suggest a close relationship between debt and retroactivity that does seem to chime with the complex dynamics of modernistic temporality.

5. Later in the text, Jünger distinguishes as follows between the ruthless partisan, who has lost all 'social hue' and operates below the level of the 'legal order', and the 'hero' proper: 'The partisan is surely a figure of the elementary but not of the heroic world. His downfall lacks a tragic quality; it transpires in a zone where one indeed maintains a dull, passive relation to pain and its secrets, but where nevertheless one is unable to rise above pain' (pp. 27–8). Once more, then, the heroic attitude to pain is born of a mixture of acceptance and transcendence.

6. Howard Caygill, *On Resistance: A Philosophy of Defiance* (London and New York: Bloomsbury Academic, 2013), pp. 125–6.

7. See Martin McQuillan, 'Extra Time and Death Penalties: the Terror of Slavoj Žižek', in his book *Deconstruction without Derrida* (London and New York: Bloomsbury Academic, 2012), pp. 171–86. Further page references will be given in the main body of the chapter.

8. Slavoj Žižek, 'Robespierre, or, the "Divine Violence" of Terror', in *Virtue and Terror (Revolutions): Maximilien Robespierre* (London: Verso, 2007). Page references will be given in the main body of the chapter.

9. While Žižek, whether or not he wishes to, is unable to decisively separate the 'radical revolutionary position' he champions from the 'fascist militarism' which *also* features a 'pre-emptive self-exclusion from the domain of the living', in his rush for a witty rejoinder McQuillan is perhaps too quick (in this moment in his essay, at least) to identify such phenomena solely with right-wing 'theocratic death cults' and then leave it at that. Of course, more widely, McQuillan's entire argument concerns the upsurge of thanatological political theology in the revolutionary discourse of some contemporary theory, but my argument suggests that *in terms of their conditions of possibility* the relationship between reaction and revolution after modernism needs more extensive thought and analysis, which pertains despite the constant temptation to evoke fascism as a self-identical or isolatable 'thing'.

10. Walter Benjamin, 'Theories of German Fascism: On the Collection of Essays *War and Warrior*, ed. Ernst Jünger', *New German Critique*, 17 (1979): 120–8. Further page references will be given in the main body of the chapter.

11. In 'Left-Wing Melancholy' Benjamin indicts the 'attitude' of a certain 'left-wing radicalism' in the interwar years, in which 'there is no longer, in general, any corresponding political action. It is not to the left of this or that tendency, but simply to the left of what is in general possible. From the beginning all it has in mind is to enjoy itself in a negativistic quiet. The metamorphosis of political struggle from a compulsory decision into an object of pleasure, from a means of production to an article of consumption – that is literature's latest hit' (*Walter Benjamin: Selected Writings Volume 2: 1927–1934*, trans. Rodney Livingstone and others, ed. Michael W. Jennings, Howard Eiland and Gary Smith (Cambridge, MA and London: Belknap Press of Harvard University Press, 1999), pp. 423–7; see p. 425). Here, for Benjamin, revolutionary potential is (as in the work of

Jünger) confounded through lack of the proper political determination and thus becomes reactionary.

12. Strauss is often thought of as an intellectual father of Neoconservatism, although some critics view this assessment of his output and influence as summary and reductive.

13. Leo Strauss, 'The Living Issues of German Postwar Philosophy', in Heinrich Meier, *Leo Strauss and the Theologico-Political Problem* (Cambridge: Cambridge University Press, 2006), pp. 115–39. Further page references will be given in the main body of the chapter.

14. In 'On Pain', as part of his critique of liberal education, Jünger writes about the loss of 'supreme authority' and its replacement by surrogate forms (pp. 20–1). Here, the text seems to engage, if obliquely, with the kind of arguments made by Weber contra Spengler. However, Jünger primarily argues for specialised training in the interests of an authoritarian state, in which discipline prevails as a form of 'contact with pain'.

15. See Gilles Deleuze, 'Coldness and Cruelty', in *Masochism* (New York: Zone Books, 1991), pp. 13–14.

16. Towards the end of his lecture, Strauss suggests that our appreciation of the philosophy of classical antiquity is nascent at best and not to be pre-judged. Preliminary attempts – for instance, Heidegger's – are just that, preliminary. In this sense, access to 'natural' philosophy is not presented as a serene prospect.

Chapter 2

Distress I

Thinking Feeling: Lyotard's Sublime

Writing on Lyotard's treatment of the Kantian sublime, Emilia Steuerman reminds us: 'The sublime for Kant is the distance between the faculty of conceiving and the faculty of presenting an object in accordance with the concept.'[1] Thus, Lyotard contends, the sublime relates to what is unrepresentable according to our faculty of understanding or cognition. It involves cases where the imagination proves itself unable to present an object that, even if only in principle, might be conceptualised as such (and where any such attempt is experienced as, in the first instance, painfully inadequate, even if it ultimately gives rise to reason's pleasures). However, Steuerman observes, for Lyotard the sublime bequeaths its legacy to modern art in two modes. The 'melancholic' (which we might associate with 'modernism') emphasises the impotence of the faculty of presentation, and is engulfed by feeble nostalgia for lost plenitude. Meanwhile, 'novatio' (which we might think of in terms of postmodernism) foregrounds, in Steuerman's terms, 'the *potency* of the faculty of conceiving which is not the faculty of understanding' (p. 114). This mode is radically inventive, giving rise to new forms of art and thinking, although, by intensifying rather than resolving a breach between the 'presentable' and the 'conceivable', 'novatio' only heightens the admixture of pleasure and pain that we associate with the sublime. 'Novatio', however, does not lament an unpresentable 'real', or allude to its properly original yet perhaps ineffable existence, but instead invents – or reinvents – the rules and discourse of unpresentability (no longer constrained by a predominating faculty of understanding) in the interests of radicalising the 'modern' precisely by exposing it to the future anterior of itself.

Coming to his *Lessons on the Analytic of the Sublime* (first published in French in 1991),[2] which provides Lyotard's most thoroughgoing explication of reflective or aesthetic judgment in Kant, we find the basis for this non-negative interpretation of the profound interplay of thought and feeling in the Kantian text. Here, Lyotard reads Kant in order to challenge the view that the third critique, the Critique of Judgment, achieves the latter's stated aim of reconciling the divisions bequeathed to philosophy by the Critique of Pure Reason and the Critique of Practical Reason taken together. Rather, Lyotard's treatment of the third critique disputes the idea that the problem of aesthetic or reflective judgment might provide the basis upon which to conceive of a permanent 'bridge' between the theoretical and the practical, arguing instead that, if read closely, the text only heightens our awareness or 'feeling' of the differend which is, at the same time, the very differend of feeling which gives rise to critical thought itself.

As Lyotard shows, in contrast to determinant judgment, if in the attempt at 'unifying philosophical knowledge' reflection is called upon in the third critique as the 'indispensable supplement' between 'understanding and reason', it nevertheless has to invent its 'own principle', to the extent that, strictly speaking, it provides less the grounds for judgment than the occasion for 'feeling', whether pleasurable or not. While, doubtless, reflective judgment is summoned in its 'heuristic capacity' in devotion to the knowledgeable procurement of 'sensations', nevertheless it is therefore fundamentally *tautegorical* to the extent that it constitutes a reflexivity without prior orientation (an orientation that only 'feeling' can make possible), judging according to a rule it gives itself but not according to concepts, thus never becoming 'an element of cognition' but instead developing, elaborating or guiding critical thought – which must be purely reflective since by definition it begins before the concept takes hold – by way of a 'manner' rather than a 'method' as such (pp. 3–4). Reflection, then, folds back or in upon itself. It is its own condition, which is also to say that it is the condition or conditions in which reflection judges its own conditions. As Lyotard puts it, 'pleasure and displeasure are at once both a "state" of the soul and the "information" collected by the soul relative to its state' (p. 4) – information which is therefore no longer about an object, but only about the 'subject' itself (whatever that may be, which indeed remains to be seen). Or, in other terms:

> Before any inquiry into the *a priori* conditions of judgments can be made, critical thought must be in a reflective state of this sort, if it does not want – and it must not want – these *a priori* conditions to be any way prejudged in its investigation. (p. 7)

To the extent that the stakes surrounding aesthetic or reflective judgment have become so high by the point of the third critique, Kant's treatment of the judging subject thus effectively becomes the propaedeutic to philosophy 'that is itself, perhaps, all of philosophy', as Lyotard puts it (p. 6). Philosophy starts out from feeling, then, in the specific sense that reflection's 'orientation' is chosen or opened 'immediately, "subjectively"' – though we will need to be extremely cautious, here, in our understanding of this term – 'in the absence of any objective criterion' (p. 8). Thus, Lyotard contends:

> if the third Critique fulfills its mission of unifying philosophy, it does so, not primarily by introducing the theme of the regulative Idea of an objective finality of nature, but by making manifest, in the name of the aesthetic, the reflexive manner of thinking that is at work in the critical text as a whole. (p. 8)

Thought's most immediate judgment upon itself – its very thought of itself – is, tautegorically speaking, sensation's other (unfounded) name. Since, in the process of such judgment, the act of thinking goes hand in hand with 'the affection that this act procures for it', such affection is just the 'inner repercussion of the act, its "reflection"' (p. 10).

While it is therefore possible to say that sensation occurs with every act of thought, and only on occasion of a thought, Lyotard counsels against any 'idea of permanence' connecting thinking and feeling within a single, stable entity, of the kind that would perhaps hazard the grounds for knowledge of a subject (pp. 10–11). For, before it is even possible to think – or, for that matter, critique – the 'subject', the act of thinking must be enjoined by a feeling that signals thought's state to itself, a state which is in fact 'nothing other than the feeling that signals it', so that, reflexively, thought thinks its state by feeling its state, by being affected by it. Such pure or immediate reflection is not the expression or the work of a subject; instead, it is simply that which gives reflective judgment its 'law'. And, as Lyotard observes: 'the notion of a "subject" in its substantive form does not seem necessary to the understanding of what reflection is. The notion of actual thought (in the sense evoked above) is sufficient' (p. 14). Thus, in this sense subjective judgment – construed as thought thinking its own 'state' by way of feeling or sensation – is not necessarily the judgment of a subject. To put it differently: 'In sensation, the faculty of judging judges subjectively' only in the sense that 'it reflects the state of pleasure or displeasure in which actual thought feels itself to be' (p. 15). It is subjective in that it has 'no objective validity', and furthermore to the extent that 'in the case of aesthetic judgment . . . the faculty of judgment' is called upon to 'judge a state' – of feeling, sensation, pleasure or displeasure – which, as Lyotard observes, is 'by this time already the judgment' (p. 15). Or, put the other way round, 'the power to critique' which under the name of reflection establishes critical philosophy as perhaps the very possibility of philosophy itself 'must have the enigmatic capacity to judge the proper conditions of judgment "before" being able to make use of . . . these conditions' (p. 31). Thus, not only does reflection *not* 'have to search for its own condition of possibility' (p. 43), it could not do so without further relapse into the tautegory that it itself is. Grounded only by means of 'the subjective formal condition of a judgment in general' (p. 16), no intrinsic demand is made upon such judgment to vindicate itself in terms of what Kant terms the 'objective reality of a concept', and for Lyotard it is this very same 'minimalism' of reflective tautegory – which in fact puts aesthetic judgment into conversation with the other faculties, in the interests of possible harmony or unification – that prevents the prior attribution of a subject as such. The subject, if there is any, is thus always in a state of infancy, a 'to-come' promised by a reflective judgment that is nevertheless always in the making – according to a temporality of 'reflection' that is, each time, singular and inventive, not emanating from a stable ground or set of conditions. In the same way, Lyotard tells us, the conditions or 'properties' which prevent the 'deduction of a sublime subject' as given or stable entity are nevertheless identical to those which permit the sublime to be 'maintained in the order of the "subjective"' (that is to say, in terms of reflective rather than determinant judgment, tautegory rather than objectivity), which, despite the dissonance that sublime feeling implies in regard to the interplay between the faculties of imagination and reason, nonetheless exercises both in relationship to one another (p. 24), in the process legitimating its apparent paradoxicality.

Nevertheless, reflection should not be understood in terms of origin or genealogy. Instead, it is simply the case that, wherever there is thought, or the possibility of thought, there is reflective tautegory. In fact, Lyotard writes: 'Much more than a genealogy, one should see in the reflexive moment a kind of *anamnesis* of critical thought questioning itself . . .' (p. 33). It is not that reflection comes first as the more original basis for other forms or orders of thought that may simply build upon it (develop, augment or supersede it as such). Rather, it is as if the unavoidable formal conditions of subjective judgment prompt persistently creative or reflexive recollection – or, in other words, self-reflection – and thus the continual re-making of thought (as irreducible to the forms of knowledge to which it bears a highly complex relationship), in the interests of what is yet to come – including the very possibility of the reconciliation of the faculties and the unification of philosophy, *to which, nonetheless, subjective judgment relates only in terms of the (feeling of) the differend.* Such 'feeling', then, orients thought on the pathway to philosophy's possible unity, at the same time as it itself only ever re-makes – rather than being able to fulfil – this same possibility (thus forever twisting or distorting what we might even *mean* by philosophy's coming to be as properly itself, or, in Lyotard's terms, its 'dwelling place').

In Lyotard's 'The Sublime and the Avant-Garde'[3] (from the early 1980s), meanwhile, whereas beauty in nature or art is characterised by the felicitous coincidence of images and concepts, sublimity arises on the strength of a certain indeterminacy which inter-implicates pleasure and pain. (In *Lessons on the Analytic of the Sublime*, of course, the distinction between pleasure and pain which in some sense suffuses and impels all of what we might term 'feeling-thought' is itself groundless to the extent that it is part of the groundless structure of reflection. As such, thought's pleasures – which is all that thought may be, or rather all that it may set out from – derive, perhaps, from a pervasive inkling or irreducible risk of pain.) While a painful blockage of expression occurs as the imagination fails to provide an adequate representation of the sublime 'object', nonetheless this makes possible pleasurable recourse to the faculty of reason as a means to contemplate the sublime, thus confirming (so it is hoped) the gratifying supremacy of rational powers. As Lyotard puts it, however, the 'dislocation of the faculties among themselves gives rise to the extreme tension (Kant calls it agitation) that characterises the pathos of the sublime, as opposed to the calm feeling of beauty' (p. 204). Thus the absolute character of the Kantian Idea, which henceforth manifests itself in a negative or even non-presentation, in fact relies on, and is in a sense produced by, something like pain, or at any rate by the agitation it helps to occasion. Since, for Lyotard, Kant's aesthetic of the sublime as described above engenders a movement away from imitative, figurative or representational painting, opening instead a pathway for minimalism and abstraction in modern art – as perhaps the privileged expression of modernity itself – it may be suggested, here, that the question of sublimity is also that of modernity's relationship to sensations of which pain is far from the least.[4]

Turning to Edmund Burke's enquiry concerning the sublime, while simply positive pleasure is obtained from what is beautiful, what is at stake in the sublime, argues Lyotard, is for Burke 'the threat of nothing further happening' (p. 204) – that is, the terror of death, of absolute privation, as another aspect of the 'painful situation' of sublimity. However, in order to create the feeling of the sublime, pleasure is reintroduced into the equation in the form of a certain suspension of terror, a lessening of the threat that may be understood as a kind of 'relief'. Nonetheless, Lyotard describes the advent of this 'relief' in terms of a particular redoubling rather than a pure cessation of the privative, since by way of the sublime in its fullest or most proper manifestation the 'soul' is deprived of the impending sense or experience of deprivation, thus undergoing privation 'at one remove'. This reading of the sublime on Lyotard's part allows him to argue that, after Burke, the sublime is 'no longer a matter of elevation (the category by which Aristotle defined tragedy), but a matter of intensification', which Lyotard also wants to describe in terms of art's capacity to return us to the always 'agitated' region between life and death in which we exist: indeed, this agitation is the soul's very 'health and its life'. By means of the sublime, death pro-foundly enters the soul – 'it is as good as dead', writes Lyotard – and yet, thanks to (sublime) art, relief, pleasure, delight, life itself returns (p. 205). That such a return takes place – that in the very midst of the impending threat of 'nothing further happening' *something happens* – is nothing less than 'shocking', Lyotard insists. The 'shock' of the modern, of modern art and perhaps modernity itself, would therefore have to do with precisely a life-after-death or life-in-death, life-death itself, that we might here associate with the sublime. That a Kantian aesthetics of the sublime is fated to engender modern artistic experiments in turn gives rise to a situation in which, for Lyotard, the 'social community' is no longer able to recognise or identify itself in terms of the aesthetic arte-facts that hitherto constituted its self-representation in various forms (p. 206). 'Art' as such thereafter abandons itself to the avant-garde, at any rate until such time as it may be ossified or monumentalised as museum exhibit – although this itself constitutes an ironic and farcical repetition, perhaps, of the privation of privation, privation 'at one remove', which announces the very onset of the sublime. Capital, too, is swept into this complex and double-edged drama, to the extent that according to Lyotard the capitalist economy constitutes a highly non-natural experiment nonetheless 'regulated by an Idea' – 'infinite wealth or power' – which, notwithstanding, it cannot manage to 'verify' by presenting any example from the so-called real world or real life (p. 209). Thus a highly antagonistic yet perhaps inseparable interplay between capitalism and the avant-garde is suggested. (In a further twist made possible by the very same logic or structure Lyotard is describing – one which makes the art market as much a feature of the Kantian legacy of the aesthetic sublime as its adversary – he argues that 'sublimity is no longer in art, but in speculation on art' (p. 210).) Such an interplay is, perhaps, just another part of this story of so-called reality becoming subjected to an increasing agitation or intensification of what we are calling 'sublime' life-death, or living death, or deathly life. Meanwhile, new artistic innovations hazard mortifying 'cynicism' to the extent that they risk merely 'the *petit frisson*, the cheap thrill, the profitable pathos, that accompanies innovation' (p. 210). Beneath this 'cynicism' Lyotard still detects 'the despair that nothing further will happen', so-called innovation railing emptily against its terrifying possibility, making something *happen* in only the most superficial sense of insisting that something has certainly happened or can be made to happen. It may be that the more fundamental task of the aesthetic sublime is to deprive us of this 'technology of time' – which is also a presumptuous 'hegemony over time' – bound up with the very 'metaphysics of capital', and thus to keep open what Lyotard calls the 'question mark of the "is it happening?"' (pp. 210–11). Such a task is, surely, at once incalculably painful (however pleasurable it may also prove to be) and intensely susceptible to the experience of life-death it is also seeking in a certain way to resist or transform.

Early in another text by Lyotard, 'Judiciousness in Dispute, or Kant after Marx'[5] (published just a year later, in 1985), the entire problematic of the aesthetic sublime bequeathed to us by Kant is linked suggestively to the seemingly intractable problem of a 'properly philosophical presentation' of thought. Lyotard gives us an image of the seventy-four-year-old Kant beset by a near-permanent head cold. Here – in a way that perhaps makes explicit some of the aspects, themes or implications of Lyotard's companion essay on the sublime and the avant-garde – feeling or 'feeling-thought' seems to acquire a body of sorts. While, for Kant, the mind through sheer effort of will has the capacity to overcome a variety of ailments, thought nevertheless causes it severe pain, a pain to which it is not just opposed, but which indeed accompanies its very operation. To the extent that this ambivalent relationship to pain is insurmountable, the ageing philosopher's inflammation of the head is linked to what Kant himself describes as an involuntary spasmodic state in the brain,[6] that is a certain inability to maintain concepts, or to secure the unified consciousness of related representations, which Lyotard wants to suggest is fundamental or necessary rather than merely contingent upon an ailment contracted late in life. Through recourse to Jean-Luc Nancy, who borrows from Kantian discourse in order to argue that any philosophical system cannot provide the direct presentation of itself required by Kant, 'since the whole is the object of an Idea which cannot be directly presented' (as Lyotard puts it (p. 325)), Lyotard suggests that philosophy's inability to present the entire 'connections which assure the maintenance of the system' (or, in other words, 'the speculative object that is the system') is not just akin to the spasmodic ailment endured by the elderly Kant, but profoundly coincident with it (p. 325). The philosopher's inability to directly present the entire grounds of a properly philosophical treatise – that is, in its manifest and apparent wholeness

– is just this spasmodic ailment of philosophy itself, one suffused with the feeling of the sublime (Lyotard might say the feeling of the differend, indeed feeling *as* differend), to the extent that it undergoes, as he himself puts it: 'first, the pleasure deriving from reason's infinite capacity to formulate an Idea (namely that of the systematic whole of thought); second, the pain born of the inability of the faculty of presentation to furnish an intuition of the Idea in philosophical discourse; and finally, the benefit arising from this disorder among the faculties' (p. 325). The latter benefit, however, does not purely and simply revive the 'transcendental illusion' through which the 'Idea' of a direct presentation of the whole system might be recuperated, since it establishes precisely the 'ontological stakes' of what is occurring philosophically here only by dint of a certain 'convulsion' which splits apart the temporal and linguistic conditions of philosophical discourse itself. Philosophy, in other words, the body of philosophy, remains sick in order to survive, ails so as to live on and thrive. Yet to the extent that it operates in contrast to the 'restful contemplation' which Lyotard sees accompanying aesthetic judgment of the beautiful, the more (philosophically) profound agitation associated with judgment of the sublime acquires a certain 'ontological advantage' by which it calls up what Lyotard here calls the 'transcendental subject' rather than just the 'empirical individual' – hence, not just seventy-four-year-old Kant with a head cold, but the philosopher or thinker *tout court*, indeed a more or less unpresentable 'subjective entity' to which Kant continues to assign 'the power of Ideas and presentations' only *as if* they were an expression of its 'human' capacities (pp. 326–7). Thus the evocation of a 'transcendental subject' as a terminological antonym in relation to the 'empirical individual' actually gives way to a sort of living-dead form of (human) being, seemingly monstrous, the semi-abortive offspring of the sublime. Indeed, Lyotard writes of the risk that, in Kant's own text, 'this "subject" is still far too heavily patterned on human experience, and that there remains much that is analogically "humanist" or anthropomorphic in what is, after all . . . a dispersion, a *Zerstreuung*, of conditions of possibility for sensation, for positive knowledge, speculation, ethics, the beautiful, the sublime' (p. 327).

Ethical Pains: Rancière's Critique of Lyotard

For several years now, Lyotard's interpretation of the Kantian sublime (and his assessment of its 'modern' importance) has been the subject of repeated critique by Jacques Rancière. For Rancière, in *Aesthetics and Its Discontents*,[7] the defining condition of aesthetic art is a severance of the grounds of 'human nature' and 'social nature', whose mutual configuration hitherto guaranteed the ordering of works of art – art's very rules – within an established set of hierarchies. With the decline of representative or mimetic forms of art, the above severance amounts to a 'gap separating nature from itself', as Rancière puts it. However, this gap (as one that interrupts the historic or projected scene of 'the world of nature fulfilling itself in culture') is also to be thought of as 'the site of an unprecedented equality' (p. 13). Aesthetic art, in which human and social nature are no longer accorded with one another, therefore calls up a new relationship between the broken hierarchies of art and a newly undifferentiated audience or public. The 'slow revolution in the forms of presentation and perception' (p. 10), about which aesthetics (less a discipline than 'the name of a specific regime for the identification of art' (p. 8)) seeks to philosophise, effectively dismantles that situation in which 'a human nature that legislates on art was tied to a social nature that determined place in society and the "sense" appropriate to that place' (p. 14).

The legacy bequeathed to us by aesthetic art and thought is therefore twofold, to the extent that it has engendered both the scandal of what is often seen as the 'anything goes' approach to artistic production, and the revolutionary promise of transformation whereby art's forms, now separated from their more conservative social operations, might powerfully contribute to 'the forms of a new life' (p. 14). In terms of this legacy, the task Rancière sets for himself is to elucidate and thereby expose an 'ethical' approach to art whose advent he sees as responsible for adversely subsuming 'art's operations' along with the political practices that it might otherwise make possible.

Of course, as Rancière notes, much of the derision accorded to aesthetic utopianism or aesthetic radicality (art's 'capacity to perform an absolute transformation of the conditions of collective existence' or to attain 'the philosophical absolute' (p. 19)) has been fuelled both by the modern history of totalitarianism and the pervasive commercialisation of art. Against this background, however, significant strands of modern thought have sought to recuperate the idea of art's singular resistance to appropriation, notably through reference to the Kantian 'sublime'. For Rancière, this happens in various ways. While some have located in the singular power of the work of art the possibility of forms of 'being-in-common' more original than those legislated for by classical or dominant concepts and practices of the 'political', others – like Lyotard – have sought to radicalise the sublime by emphasising an 'irreducible gap between the idea and the sensible', thus defining modern art as that which testifies to 'the fact of the unpresentable' (p. 20). Rancière argues, however, that in both these approaches to the sublime, what is at stake is the founding of an 'ethical community' (p. 21) on the basis of the aesthetic (whether it be one that, in his terms, celebrates the 'eucharistic host' as embodying 'the Christian power of incarnation', or one that recalls the 'Jewish prohibition on representation' exemplified by 'the burning Mosaic bush'). Such a 'community' is 'ethical', for Rancière, insofar as it is constructed upon the supposed ruins of those discourses of collective, political emancipation to which the aesthetic form of art was hitherto powerfully linked.[8] In particular, Rancière rails against those versions of the sublime, of which Lyotard's is ostensibly one, that place modern or 'avant-garde' art at an absolute distance from the everyday world. (Although the reading I gave above surely complicates somewhat this image of the avant-garde in Lyotard's writing.) As Rancière puts it, in such an aesthetics of the sublime, 'the space-time of a passive encounter with "the heterogeneous" sets up a conflict between two different regimes of sensibility'. This looks rather like the conflict between 'art' and 'non-art' (a conflict Rancière rather simplistically sees reflected by a subsidiary distinction between avant-garde and commercial art in Lyotard's work), one which he argues is 'political' in its very detachment from politics (p. 23). For Rancière, this detachment is not that of an alienation effect, replete with the 'promise-carrying contradiction' (p. 42) that paves the way for political emancipation. Instead, he argues, sublimity of the Lyotardian stripe drives modern art toward the supposedly more original 'disaster' of the human animal, its 'simple destiny of dependency' (p. 96), which binds it to an absolute alterity which can neither be reconciled nor overcome. The 'enigma' of the work, formed for Rancière by the world's contradictions, is thus lamentably recast in terms of an impossible testimony to the power of the 'Other'. (The 'avant-garde's sole responsibility is to bear the memory of it indefinitely,' writes Rancière (p. 97).) For Rancière, then, the 'ethical' task of such impossible witness thus testifies to the constitutive ruins or ruination that supposedly *is* modern art,[9] but also provides the (quasi-messianic) paradigm for keeping alive 'the memory of catastrophe' – twentieth-century 'catastrophe' in particular – without any capacity for developing new means of politics:

> This ethical dissolution of aesthetic heterogeneity goes hand-in-hand with a whole current of contemporary thought in which political dissensuality is dissolved into an archipolitics of the exception and in which all forms of domination, or of emancipation, are reduced to the global nature of an ontological catastrophe from which only a God can save us. (p. 43)

It seems that what modern art in fact bequeaths us is 'an originary and persistent tension between the two great politics of aesthetics' (pp. 43–4).

While the 'politics of resistant form' constrains the political promise of artistic experience in terms of the profound separation of the singular work, its very resistance placing a limit on the possibility of art's transformative power in terms of new forms of life, the art which devotes itself to 'becoming-life' assumes its own finality in the accomplishment of the task it sets itself: that of overcoming its own separation as such. At first, rather than simply siding with one above the other, Rancière observes that the tension between these two poles defines the current 'distribution of the sensible' in which politics and aesthetics relate to one another, at once jeopardising and making possible the aesthetic regime of art itself. For him, it is therefore a matter of conceiving the task of politics today in terms of properly understanding this tension, fully grasping the forms it might assume, and assessing its implications in terms of a potential rearrangement of the 'political' yet to come. In one sense, then, Rancière's project hesitates before simply setting aside resistant form in favour of engaged art. For one thing, the combination of the two prevents both, in different ways, from succumbing to a discourse of 'the end of aesthetics', the latter being responsible not simply for a 'disastrous captation of art' but rather a 'specific distribution of the sensible tying it to a certain form of politics' which might be conceived otherwise in future (p. 44). Nevertheless it is clear, through the tone he takes when discussing Lyotard, that Rancière detects no productive political resources of an aesthetics of the sublime, the 'resistance' of which he aligns principally with the unwanted hindrances that sublimity offers to an art oriented toward 'new forms of life'. If, to the extent that Rancière attributes to it no explicit political power that might be transformative, the aesthetic sublime is largely vestigial, largely an inert resource or a static limit in terms of the (re-)configuration of a future politics, one wonders exactly how it ever acquired or maintained its specific capacity amid the play of forces that Rancière describes in terms of the current distribution of the sensible. If Rancière indeed hesitates before simply sidelining the aesthetic sublime in favour of engaged art, it is because he recognises the complex force field in which both combine to give us the specific distribution he seeks to analyse, but if the sublime simply incapacitates (even via the forms of witness it provokes), one wonders how it might function as anything other than a mere impediment to be overcome – in which case why not simply side against it without further theoretical nuance or nicety?

Let's keep such questions open by turning to the chapter of *Aesthetics and Its Discontents* that Rancière devotes explicitly to Lyotard. Here we find Rancière's argument that, through an implicit rejection of the aesthetic nihilism of the beautiful (which in the name of culture takes nostalgic delight in civilisation's ruins), Lyotard's work expresses a preference for the 'negative task' demanded by the aesthetics of the sublime: that of witnessing the 'unpresentable'. Yet Rancière insists that, to the extent that the sublime in Kant does not refer to an art work as such but rather to the experience of imagination's incapacity before reason,[10] it places us in the domain of morality and not aesthetics. The sublime reminds reason of its superiority over nature and indeed its 'legislative vocation in the supersensible order', as Rancière puts it, thus leading out from the realm of art into 'the ethical universe' (p. 89).[11] Rancière suggests that Lyotard at once confronts and represses the consequences of this situation, by intimating that the sublime entails the sacrifice of the ethical in the domain of aesthetics, in the process giving himself to argue that the sublime is nothing less than 'the art of the disaster'. For Rancière, Lyotard twists Kant's thought such that imagination's shortcomings in the face of the sublime encourage not so much 'the autonomous law of the legislative mind' as 'subordination to the law of alterity' or heteronomy.[12] As such, the (disastrous) 'ethical' experience of the aesthetic sublime amounts to profound and insurmountable servitude to the 'Other' (pp. 93–4).

Rancière's next move is to turn to Schiller's *Letters on the Aesthetic Education of Man* as, to him, the better example of inheritance in regard to Kantian aesthetics, insofar as Schiller reveals rather than effaces their emancipatory potential. Here, Rancière argues, it becomes clear that all aesthetic experience, whether it be of the sublime or the beautiful, suspends both the law of understanding that necessitates conceptual determination and the law of sensation that entails a desired object. If aesthetic experience *tout court* thereby 'suspends the power relations which usually structure the experience of the knowing, acting and desiring subject' (p. 97), Rancière discerns in such experience freedom's promise rather than the condition of servitude. Be that as it may, since there is never simply harmonious 'agreement' of the faculties in aesthetic experience, but instead a break with any such agreement each time the aesthetic is involved, Rancière disputes the necessity of Lyotard's specific appeal to the sublime. Attraction and repulsion, agreement and disagreement, agitation and repose – for Rancière, such 'dissensual' tensions reside not merely in the sublime as a form of aesthetic experience profoundly distinct from that of the beautiful, but instead strike at the very heart of aesthetic experience as such. And as Rancière argues, it is just this dissensus that permits Schiller to attribute political capacity to the aesthetic state. For him, aesthetic experience fosters a common sense of the dissensual in that it powerfully undermines the class distinctions and hierarchies which hitherto tied art to the established order of the world, while at the same time exposing 'distant classes' to precisely the experience of their own 'distance', a distance that is nothing more than the upshot of a specific distribution of the sensible. Yet if, as Rancière argues, the aesthetic (that of the beautiful *as much as* the sublime) was always characterised by an internal movement of dissensus – as a movement that is replete with politics – then how is it possible for him to distinguish and isolate the sublime as that which encourages simply a politically conservative movement of separation, a more or less inert form of withdrawal rather than politically charged distantiation? Just as engaged art – by desiring outreach or extension to the point of its own disappearance – propels itself towards new forms of life by dint of a movement for which aesthetic experience might be another name, so surely the sublime, to the extent that it must participate in this same dissensual structure of the aesthetic, cannot be entirely emptied of transformative political capacity?

Rancière's response to this seems to be that the Lyotardian sublime is in fact anti-aesthetic, to the extent that it fails to grasp the power of the aesthetic to neutralise or displace the very conditions under which power is exercised, or the form it takes, in the order of the 'sensible' – and thus to open onto 'a new form of "sensible" universality and equality' (p. 99). Far from simply treasuring aesthetics in its isolation from the political sphere, Lyotard is, on the contrary, 'anti-aesthetics' to the extent that his 'ethical' approach neutralises the capacity of aesthetics *in* the political. And yet this same anti-aesthetics is only 'intelligible', Rancière tells us, against the backdrop of the aesthetic tension or double-bind that Schiller locates at the heart of the relationship between the Kantian faculties (one that goes so far as to establish 'the principle of a new freedom' (p. 99)). Presumably, then, such 'anti-aesthetics' are not just 'anti' pure and simple? Or, do they indeed stand against this background (one of 'true' aesthetics) as simply a blockage or impediment – even though just such a 'background' does not recognise or operate by way of simple boundary or limit (which would recall the so-called sublime 'disaster'), but according to another, more complex logic, that of dissensus? If, as Rancière implies, the 'distaster' of Lyotardian aesthetics comes about in a way that fails to recognise the contradictions at its core, then isn't it possible that Rancière's aesthetics remain trapped in just the sort of double-bind that, he argues, defines the aesthetic from the outset? While Rancière may well be happy to accede to this point about the inherent tensions of the aesthetic (albeit given his mistrust of origin stories throughout his descriptions of the ethics of 'disaster'), one wonders what it does to the 'anti' image of Lyotard with which he frequently contents himself.

As the chapter develops, Rancière states the promise or potential of the 'Schillerian primitive scene' even more starkly:

> To a humanity rent by the division of labour, occupations and ranks, it promises a community to come that no longer has to endure the alterity of aesthetic experience, but in which art's forms will again be what they once were – or what they are said to have been: the forms of unseparated collective life. Encountered within aesthetic experience, the other is no more than a self separated from itself. The alterity, or heterogeneity, which underpinned the autonomy of that experience is thereby effaced and a new alternative emerges. (p. 100)

The servile condition supposedly preserved in aesthetics of the Lyotardian stripe is overcome by the rise of a newly undifferentiated public or audience ('rent' humanity in general), bound no longer to the established hierarchies ordering artistic experience nor isolated in the disastrous experience of a separation which fails to acknowledge itself as the effect of alienation or contradiction. Thus, the 'true' other of aesthetic experience is not the absolute 'Other' of whom Rancière disparagingly speaks, but simply the 'other' of the self divided from itself in a specific distribution of the sensible, its 'otherness' overcome or superseded by the newly emergent 'forms of unseparated collected life' that hereby arise. To get to this situation nonetheless involves reasserting 'the aesthetic double-bind' by way of a 'counter-movement' or 'counter-aesthetics' that first of all restores 'aesthetic strangeness' or 'the sensible heterogeneity of aesthetic form' which 'alone carries the promise of a new sensible world' (p. 101). However, irreducible to this 'strangeness' is the effacement of the specific form that art takes (as recognisably 'art' within the existing orders of domination). Its existing borders are abolished. No longer separated from the world, or from objects of the world, the art object as no longer a distinct object is freed in terms of its 'political' capacity to reorder or reform the 'sensible'. Yet if an 'unseparated' form of collective life is potentialised by such 'counter-aesthetics', this is not simply a matter of 'conciliation' or 'reconciliation' under the sign of the One – which, as Rancière himself acknowledges, often masks domination's continued preservation. Instead, such 'collective' life is unseparated to the extent that dissensus is generalised, not least as a means to oppose an ethical consensus which neutralises political promise and accords no status to those it excludes[13] (although Rancière would distinguish such generalised dissensus from the consensual order as that which, far from seeking simply to reconcile dissensus, embodies instead 'the ultimate form of the will to absolutize this dissensus' (p. 131) in terms of the discourse of absolute respect for the other as absolutely heteronomous).

Given this, the problem with Lyotard, for Rancière, is once again that he pushes the 'irreconcilable' of the aesthetic scene to the point at which its political promise of emancipation is cancelled rather than maintained.

By the end of the chapter, the choices are stark. Separation of art of the kind Rancière associates with Lyotard's aesthetics opposes commodification without engaging its contradictions, reading into each revolutionary impulse the will to mastery, and thus arousing deep dissatisfaction with consumer culture only to speculate on the totalitarian destiny of every emancipatory politics. (If I have already questioned Rancière's simplified version of the relation of the avant-garde to the commodity in Lyotard, I will later dispute, as Lyotard himself did, this notion of the totalitarian destiny of all politics that is supposedly implied by his work.) Whereas Schillerian aesthetics frees sensory experience, for Rancière art in Lyotard's writing testifies to pure enslavement as the common condition or ground of ethical consensus and attestation. As such Lyotard leaves us with the prospect of two 'disasters': bondage to 'the immemorial law of the Other' as a consequence of the 'sacrificial announcement of the ethical in the aesthetic field' that is the sublime (Rancière takes this quotation from *The Inhuman*),[14] and the disaster of forgetting or failing to testify to this very same 'disaster', a lack of vigilance or witnessing which risks, at once, the re-emergence of totalitarianism across the political spectrum and the intensification of capitalist commodification, as two distinct yet related types of compromise or reappropriation into which all forms of aesthetic politics are inevitably swept (and which the ethical 'turn' must therefore resist or suppress). By the last chapter of *Aesthetics and Its Discontents*, the ethics of the 'Other' are read deeply into the contemporary situation of global politics. Here, since the absolute rights of the absolute victim – those powerlessly subjected to ethnic cleansing, religious persecution, sectarian warfare or other forms of extreme victimisation – have become 'the absolute rights of those without rights', it has been deemed necessary for the rights of the 'other' to be transferred to and exercised (indeed, avenged) by the 'ethical' community, for example through humanitarian intervention, international peacekeeping forces, the war on terror and so forth. For Rancière, such a situation radicalises catastrophe or 'disaster' since by dint of the 'affirmation of a state of exception' which in fact renders inoperative 'politics and right' in their classical forms, all we are left to hope for is some 'messianic' answer to despair. Yet forward-lookingness is relatively weak against the interminable memory of unrepresentable evil, of a catastrophic past extending itself seemingly endlessly into a desperate present (which is really all that calls up messianic 'hope'). Through a reading of Lyotard's 1993 lecture for Amnesty

International, 'The Other's Rights',[15] in which he sees this situation captured perfectly, Rancière argues that what opposes and seeks to violate this absolute right of the other is, for Lyotard, the will to master the unmasterable, and to thereby attain self-mastery (a 'will' in Lyotard's work that, for Rancière, takes us far too directly from the Enlightenment[16] to Revolution to Nazism). Since what is at stake in this 'will' is a refusal to bear witness to the law of the 'Other', it is therefore to be resisted, from the 'ethical' perspective, by 'infinite justice wielded against infinite evil', in Rancière's ominous phrase (p. 130) – a configuration of ethics that for him strongly suppresses the radical promise of emancipatory politics.

To the extent that, for Rancière, this ethical-consensual law of the 'Other' is also that of the 'unpresentable', one that stands guard over twentieth-century genocide from the time of Adorno onwards (in the form of an 'endless work of mourning' (p. 130)), for him what must be acknowledged is that the 'unpresentable' (an interdiction regarding representation in art, or affirmation of its impossibility) is not the only means to protest against 'the old logic' and politics of representation. Quite simply, it is a question of eliminating the 'boundary that restricts the available choice' of representations, and thus of thoroughly transforming representation itself, rather than resorting to the impossible or paralysing paradoxes of unrepresentability as such (p. 126).[17] In short, it is a matter of a new distribution of the sensible, one that, in order to realise the emancipatory promise of aesthetics and politics, must forego a Lyotardian-type 'ethical' aesthetics of sublime.

Rights of the Other

While Lyotard has of course written extensively and complexly on the sublime in a number of major texts, Rancière's condemnation of Lyotardian sublimity often revolves around just this short talk he gave as part of the Oxford Amnesty International Lectures in 1993. This occurs not just in *Aesthetics and Its Discontents* but also, for instance, in *The Politics of Aesthetics: The Distribution of the Sensible* and *Dissensus: On Politics and Aesthetics*.[18] The reference is recursive, to say the least. While this decision to repeatedly ground much larger arguments on a comparatively minor work may strike some as odd, it is therefore worth revisiting this lecture in some detail in order to evaluate properly Rancière's criticisms.

From its opening paragraph, Lyotard's lecture evokes the 'other than human' which founds the possibility of human rights. Such rights,

Lyotard argues, accrue only at the point at which 'the human is other than *a* human being', that is to say more than just basic or bare human life. As its primary historical instance, this 'other' or excess of the human is embodied in the notion of the citizen. Lyotard affirms that it is only on condition of being other-than-human that such a being may become 'an *other* human being' within the social realm of the community. 'Then "the others" can treat him as their fellow human being' (p. 136). (As Lyotard points out in a footnote which follows up on Arendt's evocation of fellow feeling in *The Origins of Totalitarianism*, in French 'fellow man' is *semblable*, which implies likeness.) If what makes human beings alike is, then, 'the fact that every human being carries within him the figure of the other' (p. 136), this 'other' emerges as the other-than-human in the other human that I also am. As such, it arises not as some primeval origin, divine enigma or source of ancient debt. Instead, it is simply the foundational situation of citizenry in general, which – in a way that is surely not entirely remote from Rancière's thinking of dissensus – Lyotard formulates outside of notions of the absolute identity of the social bond.[19] (One implication of such citizenry as it occurs in Lyotard, of course, is that one never attains 'full' citizenship pure and simple, citizenship without remainder, since the figure of the citizen is also that of the '*other than*', meaning that human lives can never be unproblematically reduced to the citizen-form to which they nevertheless tend.)

Lyotard probes further the question of 'what is this figure of the other in me?' His answer, following Arendt, is 'nothing but a man', or, even more minimally, 'nothing other than an individual of the species Homo sapiens' (p. 136). While throughout this lecture Lyotard indulges in what we might now view as a rather hasty contrast between the instinctual and sensory communication of the 'animal' and the non-instinctual operations of human language, his thinking of the conditions of speech is what is most important here. For Lyotard, the communicability which underpins human interlocution is characterised by a certain heterogeneity, in that human language entails forms of address which are necessarily dissymmetrical: I speak, you listen (and, alternately, vice versa). While animals can instinctively and sensorily 'merge into a community based on signals', the very circumstances of interlocution mean that human beings cannot (p. 138). Thus, what in one sense founds human community (the other-than-human in me which makes me an-other human) also establishes the frontiers of communal identity, or in other words the limit of the community's integrity or coherence as such. It does so precisely to the extent that what founds civil life is the heterogeneity and dissymmetry which grounds the operations of language or speech construed as a form of address to another. It is only with the reduction of the human being to bare life, or in other words the fall into complete non-citizenship, that the principle of heterogeneity established by human language is diminished. Or, rather, vice versa, as Lyotard puts it: 'only when the impossibility of interlocution' arises are we reduced 'to that meager resource' (p. 138). Consequently, just such a human '*we*' is therefore a product or condition of human interlocution rather than the origin that founds its possibility. This is not to imply, since language and community do not derive from a prior human 'we' or an essential 'humanity', that the origin of the 'human' is non- or inhuman in the form of some divine or primordial Other to whom we are therefore impossibly indebted. Instead it simply affirms that the 'other' in me and in the other, which founds the possibility of human communicability and citizenry, is the necessary supplement to that possibility itself. It is not in any simple sense previous or external to but coterminous with the making of civil life (the temporality of which, as we shall see, is nonetheless no less heterogeneous than its form of communication).

For Lyotard, then, 'the citizen is the human individual whose right to address others is recognized by those others' (p. 138). The formulation of the human being as other-than-human/an-other-human, routed through the dissymmetry or heterogeneity of interlocution, is not equated with a law of the Other that is in any simple sense prior to or outside of the 'human', as its 'divine' or mystical origin. Instead, it is explicitly linked to the specific historical forms that civil society *will have taken*, entering in as a decisive yet non-integratable element (that is, non-assimilable and yet indispensable to both the language and the time of civility). If the principle of the right to address the other, and of the other's recognition of this right, founds the historical possibility of human society in its modern sense, whether it be 'the Greek *politeia* or the modern *republic*' (p. 138), this possibility profoundly partakes of the future anterior, to the extent that in its very form or structure the 'model' cannot be spatially closed or temporally frozen since the heterogeneity which permits the interlocution of citizenry places a limit on the community's coherence, stability and identity (in other words, on what Rancière would perhaps call consensus), thus opening onto other possibilities, other futures, other forms of 'human' organisation and interaction, for good or ill. Nonetheless, Lyotard asserts that while the social and geopolitical extension of civility may be promoted, restricted or otherwise managed by various means (of which there are many examples throughout history: 'an obligatory single language, an official language alongside which traditional languages are tolerated, compulsory multilingualism, effective multilingualism, and so on'), ultimately such strategies only determine how interlocution eventually extends, rather than being able to quell its extension more radically (p. 140).

Amid model social forms, it is for Lyotard the 'republican principle' in particular which introduces 'civic interlocution' into the community, and which therefore maintains the principle of heterogeneity or alterity in the realm of human communication. Without it, he suggests, the 'demos' or 'demotic' in its pure form risks a fall into absolute consensuality. For Lyotard it is the 'nation' (presumably in its most 'nationalistic' form) which in modern terms most recalls such a situation. Here, alterity is excluded through a process of non-recognition in which the excluded is precisely not recognised as an other (Rancière would presumably have trouble disputing this analysis of exclusion since he frequently reminds us of it). Now, for Lyotard, the republican principle is avowedly 'contractual'. As such, the 'other' it maintains within the social form that the community takes is not that of an ancient or divine law preceding human sociability and interlocution in absolute terms. Instead, it arises on the strength of a 'civil' agreement between humans concerning the right to speech and the radical dissymmetry of address – even if, amid the heterogeneity of civil 'time', such an 'other' facilitates (and indeed puts at risk) that agreement as much as epitomising it. (Put differently, in a multiple and heterogeneous sense the other is the very 'making' of civility – and very possibly its 'breaking' too.) I have the right to address you, and you me, a right established prior to any inkling that we may agree. Hence the heterogenous time of the 'civil', which makes its agreement prior to the very possibility of agreement. Indeed, what binds 'us' is that *on principle* we may never be bound by anything other than the principle enshrined in the republican 'contact' – that of heterogeneous speech and dissymmetrical address, to which we will have unconditionally agreed without having agreed to it.

It is in light of these remarks that Lyotard evokes the 'forgotten', a term upon which Rancière dwells in order to mount his increasingly florid critique of Lyotardian thought as perhaps the most hyperbolic form of poststructuralism's discourse of the other. Here, though, the term arises in the context of a fairly down-to-earth explanation of Amnesty's precise vocation, which Lyotard is careful not to inflate or overstate, describing it as 'minimal' and yet 'decisive' precisely within the limits of its own specificity:

> *Amnestos* meant he who is forgotten. Amnesty does not demand that the judgment be revised or that the convicted man be rehabilitated. It simply asks that the institution that has condemned him to silence forget this decree and restore the victim to the community of speakers. (p. 141)

While Lyotard does not say as much, logically speaking the restoration of interlocutory relations and rights might not just mean release without question. It might also take the form of a fair trial, proper rights and conditions in prison, insistence upon the legal accountability of the state and so forth. To recall the forgotten in such contexts does not so much appeal to some primordial law of the Other, but first of all reaffirms the fundamental principle of the civil contract. 'The others rights', to reprise Lyotard's title, are in this sense not those of some absolutised Other, but refer instead to those rights which makes the 'civil' possible, possible among all of 'us' (rights which would seem especially important since, however it may be determined, the extension of the 'civil' cannot be curbed).

To the extent that remembering the forgotten is, here, the particular task of Amnesty as a human rights organisation, such recollection is therefore less a matter of hyperbolic melancholy or paralysing obligation, testifying to itself in the enigmatic name of an absolute Other. Instead, perhaps more prosaically (or rather, more 'minimally' yet 'decisively'), Amnesty's task of vigilant non-forgetting is 'in accordance with the provisions of the public law of the republican democracies' (p. 141) – that is, law founded on the right to speech and the capacity of address. The law of the republic establishes duty as much as right, yet such duty is not the debt of the absolute *arche*, but occurs instead because the right of the human being as other-than-human/an-other-human is by definition not natural, and is therefore 'merited' or earned through civilisation, or in other words through the education or instruction that the civil contract promises.

Within this model of interlocutory civility, silence does not commemorate the 'Other' as the absolute resource of a pure enigma. It is simply the condition of possibility of address. It is only through recognising the value of his own silence before the teacher's address that the pupil in his turn earns the right to speak (in a phrase that the Rancière of *The Ignorant Schoolmaster*[20] must have blanched at, Lyotard argues that 'the exaltation of interactivity as a pedagogic principle is pure demagogy' (p. 142)). The pupil's silence, in other words, teaches the value of the right to speak. It is here, for the first time in Lyotard's own discourse, that the Other with a capital 'O' comes into play, for the teacher as master is 'not the figure of the general other, of you, but the figure of the *Other* in all its separateness' (p. 142). But Lyotard confers this big 'O' on the otherness of the master-teacher only in the sense that, in contrast to the citizen in general, what the master-teacher has to say is not so easily reducible to 'interlocutory expectation' (p. 142). The discourse offered by the master-teacher conveys things that the pupil does not already know and may not, indeed may never, understand. Thus this form of speech more radically *estranges* – although, of course, it does not simply threaten to destroy the community, far from it, since what is estranging about pedagogic language also profoundly confirms the alterity or heterogeneity at the core of the civil contract, i.e. the right of the other's address, so that the teacher from this perspective becomes as much the cornerstone of civil life as the stranger or foreigner in 'our' midst (although such a teacher is, equally, far from just the conservative guardian of 'what is'). Rather than entailing some mysterious rite of the uncommunicable, the estranging communication of such an 'Other' may be the only kind truly worthy of its name, since to communicate something fully communicable is precisely to tell someone something they are already capable of knowing or understanding, and that in a sense they therefore already 'know'. In a more fundamental sense, this would obviously be no sort of communication at all. As Lyotard puts it here, if nothing is 'announced', if there is no innovation in the content or for that matter no inventiveness at the level of form, we are doomed to 'repetition and to the conservation of existing meanings' (p. 143). The right to speak (which is also, as we have seen, a duty) is just this duty to announce. It comes with a demand to estrange, that is to instruct. However, for all its quasi-religious resonance, such 'announcement' is not so much redolent of the voice of God, of the mystical force of sovereign edict, or of spiritual testimony and conviction; it is simply that which attests in the civil contract to the republican principle of the right to speech. Indeed, in this sense while it is far from based on a simple principle of all-levelling equality 'announcement' offers itself as a prime source of resistance to the consensus that deadens, silences or excludes. As Lyotard puts it, through the repetition and conservation of existing meanings human community even as it 'spreads' will 'remain the same, prostrated in the euphoria it feels at being on such very good terms with itself' (p. 143), unless it is given to instruction as the very counterpart to speech rights.

Indeed, such estranging communication beyond 'interlocutory expectation' is also a matter of 'speaking otherwise than is my wont and saying something other than what I know how to say' (p. 142). It thus estranges the teacher as much as the pupil from himself. But this does not make it some absolute resource of a primeval Other, merely the more radical condition of possibility at the heart of the interlocutory situation of civil life, indeed of the very right to speech that it always accompanies or supplements, however unstably (such instability being its necessary element, of course). Again, then, far from being the catastrophic Other construed as absolutised origin of ethical consensus or testimony, Lyotard's 'Other' is more accurately here the guarding-opening site of resistance to 'the interlocutory consent of the community', inscribed specifically within the (always unstable) historical formation of the civil contract. Since the term ethics crops up here it is important to note, as Bill Readings once observed, that the 'ethical' in Lyotard arises at the point where 'instances of dispute conventionally determined as political are seen to be more justly considered as sites for indeterminate judgment',[21] or in other words judgment without given criteria. While Rancière would no doubt align the ethics which arise from Lyotard's reading of Kant – and for that matter Levinas – with a foreclosure of the project of political emancipation, nonetheless such ethics are not the basis on which to securely found a consensual community (of testimony) in the sense that communicative consensus is always 'wagered against the differend', as Readings puts it (p. 120), while to the extent that indeterminate judgment always judges in a form that falls short of reconciling incommensurable interests or claims, it leaves the differend exposed and testifies to the openness of the question 'what is happening?' (p. 124).

If the silence endured by the pupil, or for that matter the writer or the monk (to use Lyotard's examples of the 'separated'), entails a necessary degree of suffering, this is not so much an agonising facet of originary disaster, then, but once more a condition of the civil contract, an intrinsic if unsettling feature of the right and duty of speech. Such pain or harm as is done by silence becomes a wrong only at the point it is denied speech in turn, and it is this that Lyotard here means by testimony. As such, the testimony of which Lyotard speaks does not testify to the 'disaster' in the specific form it is evoked by Rancière, far from it; by testifying to its pain or harm, such witness in fact attests to the civil contract and the right and duty of speech as the historic promise of human being (in the form of the 'other-than-human/an-other-human').

Now, all of this brings us to Lyotard's treatment of the Nazi concentration camps in the concluding pages of his talk. For Lyotard, the 'extermination' that occurred in the camps may be thought of as, among other things, a terrible violence done to the civic or 'republican' contract. It is, in other words, an extreme offence against the right of speech. It is in the specific sense that the camps involved a situation characterised by a terrible deprivation of the right to speech on the part of the victims, and what would seem to be a radical emptying-out of the very possibility of announcement or instruction that forms its indispensable corollary, that we are left with the dilemma of how to communicate the abjection of the camps. In this double sense, then, the extermination was first and foremost a 'severing of communication', the utter extinguishing of address. 'The terror of what it means no longer to be destined to anyone or anything', as Lyotard puts it (p. 144), using the term 'destined' not to suggest some religious destiny, for instance that of the Jews, but instead to evoke the violent and irrevocable ending of the destinal or, in other words, destruction of the constitutive possibility of address that gives us the 'civil'. (The 'destinal' always includes as a necessary feature of its possibility the chance that the message sent by addresser to addressee may not arrive, as Lyotard's entire discourse here suggests. This is what Derrida would call 'destinerrance'. Here, the structural inscription of such destinerrance within the rights of speech as a condition of civil life warns us against confusing Lyotard's allusion to destiny with an idea of the historic fate of the Jews, not least in the 'catastrophic' form Rancière attributes to Lyotardian thought.)

If the death camps confound what Lyotard calls 'interlocutory expectation', nevertheless on the basis of his 1993 Amnesty lecture it is still possible to imagine communicability's radical demand of announcement or instruction renewing itself in the face of such horror, precisely by calling us to speak of what we don't know, requiring us to say what we don't know how to say and to hear what we can't understand. In this situation, Lyotard's statement that 'our debt to announcement can never be acquitted' does not merely imply radical silence befalling an insuperable catastrophe, to which testimony is through an impossible obligation thereafter hopelessly bound (as Rancière might have it). Rather, it quite simply recalls to us the rights and duties of civil life. When Lyotard writes that 'the Other in language, the Other that language is, does not say what must be said' (p. 145), this can be interpreted to mean that the master-teacher, as embodiment or epitome of the 'Other', must always earn the right to speak, to announce or instruct anew, through keeping a certain silence (that of the pupil or citizen-to-be), a silence which nevertheless unsettlingly recalls the profound silencing of the victims. A silence which may in fact permeate all that he will thereafter say, all that may be said. Perhaps most demandingly, the interlocution of the teacher must grapple with the fact that the one to whom the Other announces is by definition kept silent by his very speech, kept in silence by instruction, recalling the silencing of the victims of the camp. This 'must' be said, although by definition the situation to which it refers cannot be completely 'said' or fully included in speech. If all interlocution risks the suffering of the other, even as it confers rights and establishes duties, it is above all the Other's speech that risks suffering of the unspeakable kind, even as it remains at the heart of the civil promise. Thus it is that the Other risks his own unspeakable suffering: 'Even those who submit themselves to the ascesis of separation in order to exalt the annunciatory power of language run the risk of abjection' (p. 145). They must in a sense betray themselves through a fearful complicity with what is foreign to the interlocutory community and, as such, must place themselves in the ambivalent and abject position of the 'sacred': that is, the position of the one who is excluded from the 'speech community', one who is none-theless capable of leaving a most fearful mark, at the extremes of legibil-ity or intelligibility. Thus it is that, through the impossibility of acquittal, announcement includes the 'unforgettable' of the 'forgotten' (pp. 144–5). This has little to do with ancient gods, arche-origins or testimony to a quasi-religious law; it concerns instead the always divided historical formation of the civil contract. It has to do with civil life as fundamen-tally and necessarily unstable, prone to the other of itself in a double sense that is as dangerous as it is promissory.

Contrary to what one might expect from Rancière, it is only in the very last pages that the sublime is mentioned, in fact only once, where it is the Burkean sublime that is evoked to describe the horror of a person whose capacity to take part in speech is jeopardised. Since the power that represents such a threat quells interlocution, it cannot be joined in dialogue. It cannot be figured as a 'you', and thus it exceeds any human determination (or for that matter, any identity, be it divine or animal). Since this power is also that of the Other, Lyotard offers a further reminder that, while its 'mastery' constitutes an indispensable yet dis-symmetrical element of the civil contract, the Other cannot be mastered or appropriated as such. Thus the sublime is alluded to here only to foreground, once more, both the underlying conditions and the inherent fragility of the modern socius (and not some primeval enigma). Mention of the sublime provides an opportunity, not for melancholic reflection or paralysing lament, but for the acknowledgement that 'the effort of trans-lation must be endlessly renewed' (p. 146). This effort would correspond to both the impossible task of appropriating the Other's power (which, unfeasible as it may be, would result in the terror of absolute consensus), and the injunction to negotiate 'otherwise' the borderline between announcement and the right to speak, on the one hand, and the onset of silence and the 'night' (as Lyotard puts it), on the other. For Lyotard, republics arise from 'triumphant identification with the Other', which also entails precisely the possibility of 'terror' (a 'terror' which, as an effect of just such an openness to the 'Other', comes much less from Enlightenment attempts at self-mastery or overcoming 'otherness' than Rancière's reading of Lyotard would have it). Yet despite this possibility Lyotard does not hesitate to say that we are 'afflicted' today by attempts to foreclose the Other. This double recognition – of the terror and promise of the Other – indicates both Lyotard's resistance to the idea of an ethical-consensual community and his understanding of the complex stakes of the civil project itself.

Lyotard's lecture concludes by returning to the theme of the pupil as child, the one who does not yet speak, who is not yet an interlocutor even though he is an integral part of the interlocutory exchange that forms the basis of the civil community. As a condition of the possibility of his own speech, a speech still to come, the child acknowledges the other's right to speak only through the instruction of the Other, before whom he is mute, and whose discourse may well be unintelligible to him, even though he hears and accepts it. Unable to articulate his most infant response to the Other's injunction, the capacity and entitlement to speak which he learns (and earns) is forever shot through with this impediment, the interlocutory deficit of the Other's law that enacts the right to speech. As such, the 'mute distress' which pertains to the situation of the *infantia* remains after 'our native prematurity' (p. 147) is over, precisely since we owe to this very same 'distress' the ability to speak and to question, as well as the capacity to be welcomed and acknowledged within civil life as 'other-than-human/an-other-human'. The intensely ambivalent power of the Other as source of highest promise and deepest peril pervades our civil identity before it is properly made, indeed in its very making and continual re-making (once more, heterogeneity characterises the time as much as the language of the citizen). Or, as Lyotard puts it: 'I have to announce to you the opaque Otherness that I have experienced, and still am experiencing, as a child . . . the law that forbids the crime of abjection nonetheless evokes its abiding threat or temptation' (p. 147). 'Distress' is at the origins of civil life, then, precisely to the extent that such distress is an indispensable element in its very make-up.

The Distress of Rancière-Lyotard

Solely on the basis of this close reading of Lyotard's lecture, as one that places a radically non-consensual form of citizenship at its very centre, the antagonism that characterises Rancière's attitude to Lyotard is surely in need of further explanation. Or, rather, we would need to present Rancière's hostility differently than Rancière himself does, since clearly Lyotard's discourse cannot so simply be reduced to some sort of mystical reverence for a primordial Other which produces itself as quasi-religious obstacle to the onward march of political emancipation. Of course, the background to Rancière's animosity is much more complicated, having to do with Lyotard's infamous yet undeniably complex critique of Marxism, his stance on the Gulf War of the early 1990s, his opinions on avant-garde art (which Rancière undoubtedly simplifies), his attitude to anti-demagogic or anti-populist forms of teaching which, at first glance at least, conflict strongly with those found in Rancière's *The Ignorant Schoolmaster*, and his appeal to the differend which from a certain perspective may be seen to delegitimise the taking of sides in a situation of struggle. Overall, there is – superficially at least – much in Lyotard for anyone who is committed to a certain idea of emancipation to object to. However, the criticisms levelled at 'The Other's Rights' are probably really aimed at other texts by Lyotard, notably *The Inhuman* and, perhaps even more so, *Heidegger and 'the jews'*,[22] written just a few years earlier than the Amnesty lecture. While admittedly the latter book includes some passages that allow translation and interpretation of the kind that fuels Rancière's offensive, it also contains others that require such an attack to be at the very least more complexly grounded. In particular, Rancière mistakes the differend of 'the jews' in the history and thought of the Occident (i.e. 'the jews' as an undominatable and undomesticatable element 'irremissible in the West's movement of remission and pardon', as Lyotard writes in *Heidegger and 'the jews'* (p. 22), thus inappropriable to its language and its time) for what he sees as Lyotard's uncritical *identification* with a 'Jewish' law of the Other. '"The jews" are not tragic, they are not heroes', says Lyotard (p. 28) – thus it is not that their separation is tragically or heroically constituted (as the source of a valorising identification). Lyotard is very clear on this point. He goes on to write:

> I am emphasizing the gap just so that one stops inundating us (?) with the notion of 'Judeo-Christianism' – which is fashionable nowadays after Auschwitz, a way of conserving the horror by repressing it, where the forgetting of the forgotten, of the Other, persists. (p. 39)

By restoring the differend of 'the jews' in place of the politically and ideologically charged hyphen that joins the Christian and the Jew, Lyotard does not so much desire heroic separation, but rather seeks the 'grounds' of opposition to a certain form of forgetting, one which only the Other (no doubt the Other of 'us', the non-consensual Other of 'The Other's Rights') can resist. In other words, this passage can be read in terms of the thinking that we have already seen emerge from the 1993 lecture by Lyotard, rather than in the light of Rancière's rather caricatured reading of Lyotard. It is indeed in these terms (i.e. the Other as the resistant limit of consensual terror) that the following remark by Lyotard becomes legible: 'Today, hatred comes softly as integration of "the jews" into a permissive collectivity in the name of the "respect for differences," well known and recognized, between the "ethnocultural" components of what remains of the old modern nations' (p. 39). On the basis of a closer reading (one that he himself forgoes), Rancière would probably have a hard time assimilating such critical comments about the grounds of ethical 'toleration' to the terms of his own critique of Lyotard. Meanwhile, in another section of *Heidegger and the 'jews'*, the impossible witnessing of the Other 'after Auchwitz' (in art, writing and elsewhere) gives rise to a 'more "archaic" anxiety', one that is 'precisely resistant to the formation of representations' only in the sense that this anxiety entails 'displacement of the tasks of secondary repression onto the sociocultural apparatuses' which themselves reveal 'the sickness that Freud prophesied would increase with "civilization"' (p. 48). No doubt for Rancière there is much to object to here, in terms of the limit this analysis sets on emancipatory optimism. But the point is that Rancière's tactic of dismissing such analysis by evoking some paralysing quasi-religious aura pervading Lyotard's writings can easily be put in question through a more complex consideration of what is at stake in this allu-sion to 'secondary repression' (in contrast to the mythical forgetting of primary repression, the latter entails a more concrete act of repression whereby once-conscious ideas or perceptions are forcefully expelled from consciousness). Secondary repression may well put 'us' in thrall of the unforgotten-forgotten, making the stakes of a political transfor-mation of 'civilization' all the more complicated, but it does not imply the unshakeable grip of primordiality. As Bill Readings once succinctly noted, the 'immemorial' in Lyotard is that which:

> can neither be remembered (represented to consciousness) nor forgotten (con-signed to oblivion) . . . the immemorial acts as a kind of *figure* for conscious-ness and its attempts at representing itself historically. The prime example is Auschwitz . . .[23]

Acting as a kind of *figure* – one must highlight such phrasing, since it has an important theoretical resonance throughout Lyotard's work – the immemorial names at once a 'historical' differend and, perhaps more crucially, the (unclosable) differend of the historical, recognition of which underlies the project of an always ongoing refiguration of the politics of representation which would be the precondition for 'politics' as such. Or, as Lyotard writes in *Heidegger and 'the jews'*:

> At this point I enter into what really concerns us, historians and nonhisto-rians. A past that is not past, that does not haunt the present, in the sense that its absence is felt, would signal itself even in the present as a specter, an absence, which does not inhabit it in the name of full reality, which is not an

object of memory like something that might have been forgotten and must be remembered (with a view to a 'good end,' to correct knowledge). (p. 11)[24]

Here, the memory of 'the jews' is not simply aligned with the calling of some ancient or mythical Other inscribed in terms of an original lack or prohibition which grounds ethical testimony with a view to the 'good end', but is instead, if anything, the complex after-effect of the concrete exclusions of 'secondary repression'. And if 'no revolutionary program [can] find a place in the tradition of "the jews"' (p. 37) it is not simply because Judaism comports a more original law in terms of which the logic of revolution is always already ruled out as part of its divine code, but rather because 'the jews' point to a differend in the very make-up of the West (a differend felt, for instance, in the experience of the sublime) which puts in question revolutionary possibility pure and simple.

One could extend this series of quotations in the interests of a more nuanced approach to Lyotard's book on Heidegger and 'the jews', which is admittedly sufficiently theoretically dense and complex to be potentially combustible in terms of its possible readings. One might also examine carefully Lyotard's own rebuttal of the criticism levelled against him during the 1980s, namely that his writing – to borrow Lyotard's own phrasing of his opponents' point of view – leaves 'no antidote to totalitarianism other than a politics of terror' (a criticism that doubtless differs from Rancière's, but which nonetheless resonates in its attempt to at once totalise and neutralise – that is to *disaster-ise* – the 'political' dimension of Lyotard's thought).[25] But I hope I have demonstrated in sufficient detail the comparative lack of rigour and sophistication that accompanies Rancière's engagement with Lyotard (or, more properly speaking, the *displaced* nature of Rancière's repeated criticisms) to be able to break off from any further attempt to adjudicate their relations, in favour of raising the somewhat larger question of how to characterise the Lyotard–Rancière 'dispute' itself: that is, in terms of the precise form it takes. Is it the case that 'Lyotard' and 'Rancière' (as names for two forms or ways of thinking) relate to one another only according to the logic of the differend or by dint of a language game through which, in order for one to speak, the other must stay mute – a 'game', in others words, whereby what authorises (and yet problematises) the address made by each is the demand of the other's silence? Or is this relation differently 'distressed', not by some uncrossable gulf of the differend but instead by a yet more complex set of interactions characterised both by differentiation and deferral, for which another name might be *différance* (a *différance* which perhaps occasions hyperbolic denunciation of the 'other' in displaced form, à la Rancière)? Just as I have suggested moments in the 'text' of both Lyotard and Rancière where the absolute difference of the two is somewhat undermined, so one might point for instance (as Rancière himself does, albeit in a highly qualified way) to the uneasy 'common ground' between Rancière's own notion of the 'democratic paradox' and what he terms Derrida's enquiry into the aporetic structure of democracy, in order to further entangle the 'deconstructive' and 'Marxist' traditions we are given to inherit. In the essay to which I am alluding here, 'Does Democracy Mean Something?',[26] Rancière opposes the democratic practice of dissensus to what he describes as the Derridean aporia of democracy. Interestingly, in order to criticise the limits of Derrida's concept of democracy Rancière resorts to rehashing his critique of Lyotard (the 1993 Amnesty lecture rears its fateful head once more!). While Rancière is quick to maintain some differences between Derrida and Lyotard (the former apparently being more interested than the latter in the emancipatory qualities of 'messianic promise' rather than 'obedience to the Law'), predictably enough both are identified with and indeed reduced to 'an ethical overstatement of otherness' (p. 60). 'Does Democracy Mean Something?' may therefore be read in terms of the complexly disposed relations and resources of Marxism and deconstruction, which vie uneasily here: Leftism of the Rancierian stripe contends with the deconstruction that it also acknowledges in part, while, as part of the same critical movement, deconstruction (in its two different versions) is acknowledged to be not quite itself, albeit a 'self' that comes down to the same thing in the end. (If such would be the Rancièrian logic here, one could imagine a 'deconstructive' rejoinder that imagined the complexity of these processes of deferral and differentiation somewhat differently.) Whether the relationship of 'Rancière' to 'Lyotard' is to be understood in terms of the 'distress' of the differend (or, put otherwise, the dissymmetry of instruction and address that here repeats the severance of emancipatory politics from an ethics of the other), or whether it is to be thought of in terms of the pained agitation occasioned by *différance* (that is, of a differentiation which cannot fully repress deferral) one hesitates to see how its language games open on to the pure optimism of 'dissensus'.[27] Put more bluntly, one implication of my argument is that Rancière may well portray Lyotard somewhat cartoonishly (that is reductively, simplistically, in displaced form) because he simply does not want Lyotard's 'politics' to have anything to say, either to 'us' or to him, Rancière himself. Why not? One would have to ask further about the 'politics' of Rancière to answer this. But the 'distress' I detect underlying Rancière's position is also that of a desire to resist the sublime as constitutive of a pure impediment to emancipatory politics, a desire which knows it threatens to delegimitise other aspects of the very same project or analysis – by which I refer to the double gesture on Rancière's part of, on the one hand, a refusal of the sublime (as) blockage itself, and, on the other, the semi-repressed inclusion of the sublime within a 'Schillerian' aesthetics of emancipation.

Notes

1. Emilia Steuerman, 'Habermas vs Lyotard: Modernity vs Postmodernity?', in *Judging Lyotard*, ed. Andrew Benjamin (London: Routledge, 1992), pp. 99–118. See p. 113. Further references will be given in the main body of the chapter.
2. Jean-François Lyotard, *Lessons on the Analytic of the Sublime*, trans. Elizabeth Rottenberg (Stanford: Stanford University Press, 1994). Further page references will be given in the main body of the chapter.
3. Jean-François Lyotard, 'The Sublime and the Avant-Garde', in *The Lyotard Reader*, ed. Andrew Benjamin (Oxford: Basil Blackwell, 1991), pp. 196–211. Further page references will be given in the main body of the chapter.
4. While it crops up quite a bit in the texts under discussion, it is nevertheless important to be a little wary in using the terminology of the 'modern' in relation to Lyotard, since as is well known he cautions against any chronologistic usage of the term, notably in relation to the 'postmodern'. Far from constituting discreet and successive or consecutive periods of time, the 'modern' and the 'postmodern' are thus made up of conditions that relate complexly (and non-sequentially) in regard to one another.
5. Jean-François Lyotard, 'Judiciousness in Dispute, or Kant after Marx', in *The Lyotard Reader*, pp. 324–59. Further page references will be given in the main body of the chapter.
6. Lyotard here cites from Kant, *Werke*, 6 (Frankfurt: Insel-Verlag, Wilhelm Weischedel), pp. 389–90. (The reference is to *The Conflict of the Faculties*.) The translator Cecile Lindsay adds a note to say that, while the author's references to the German edition have been followed, the standard English translation of the Kantian texts cited has been used.
7. Jacques Rancière, *Aesthetics and Its Discontents*, trans. Steven Corcoran (Cambridge: Polity, 2012). Further page references will be given in the main body of the chapter.
8. Rancière makes such arguments, with varying degrees of nuance, across a number of his texts. They often centre on Lyotard, where critical intensity tends to heighten. Indeed, Rancière is clearly fond of reprising his critique of the Lyotardian sublime, finding subtle ways to reiterate acrimonious dissatisfaction. See, for instance, the Foreword to *The Politics of Aesthetics: The Distribution of the Sensible*, trans. Gabriel Rockhill (London and New York: Continuum, 2004), and those sections of the chapter on 'Artistic Regimes and the Shortcomings of the Notion of Modernity' in which the comments included in the Foreword are further worked out (see esp. p. 29). See also, for example, *Dissensus: On Politics and Aesthetics*, trans. Steven Corcoran (London and New York: Continuum, 2010), esp. pp. 59–60,

72–4, 182. Here, across a series of different essays Rancière's rancour gathers itself, as will be seen, through repetitive focus on Lyotard's 1993 lecture for Amnesty International, 'The Other's Rights'. This is a text we will therefore go on to read closely.

9. To be more specific regarding Lyotard, in *Aesthetics and Its Discontents* Rancière argues as we shall see that Lyotard contrasts the 'positivistic nihilism of aesthetics as a discourse which, under the name of culture, delights in the ruined ideals of a civilization' with just this 'negative task' of bearing impossible witness to the 'unpresentable' (p. 89).

10. Although Rancière argues otherwise, Lyotard of course knows this. For instance, in *Heidegger and 'the jews'* (Minneapolis: University of Minnesota Press, 1990) he writes: 'Art is an artifact; it constructs its representation. Art cannot be sublime; it can "make" sublime . . .' (p. 45). While, on this basis, there would be much to say about his characterisation of Lyotard's 'mistaken' thinking about the sublime, if nothing else it points to Rancière's haste in wanting to present a reductive image of the Lyotardian project.

11. In *The Future of the Image*, Rancière describes the 'ethical turn' with which he is concerned in *Aesthetics and Its Discontents* in terms of 'a Platonic ethical framework that does not involve the notion of art, but where what is judged is simply *images*, where what is examined is simply their relationship to their origin (are they worthy of what they represent?) and their destination (what effects do they produce on those who receive them?)' (Rancière, *The Future of the Image*, trans. Gregory Elliott, London and New York: Verso, 2007, p. 111). See, though, my note 10 above.

12. In the final essay included in *Aesthetics and Its Discontents*, 'The Ethical Turn of Aesthetics and Politics', Rancière argues that through his reading of the Kantian sublime Lyotard twists ethics into the very law of aesthetics whereas, in Kant, it opens a pathway out of the realm of art, so that in the process aesthetic freedom and Kantian moral autonomy are together overturned by and twisted into the (ethical) monster of art's heteronomy, its subjection to the law of the 'Other' (see esp. pp. 127–8). In similar vein, in *The Future of the Image*, when discussing Lyotard, Rancière writes: 'The problem of "sublime art" is thus posed in simple terms: one cannot have sublimity both in the form of the commandment prohibiting the image and in the form of an image witnessing the prohibition. To resolve the problem, the sublime character of the commandment prohibiting the image must be identified with the principle of a non-representative art. But in order to do that, Kant's extra-artistic sublime has to be identified with a sublime that is defined within art. This is what Lyotard does when he identifies Kant's moral sublime with the poetic sublime analysed by Burke' (p. 132). Again, see my notes 10 and 11 above.

13. See Rancière, *Aesthetics and Its Discontents*, pp. 115–16.

14. Jean-François Lyotard, *The Inhuman*, trans. Geoffrey Bennington and Rachel Bowlby (Cambridge: Polity, 1993) p. 137.

15. Jean-François Lyotard, 'The Other's Rights', in *On Human Rights*, ed. Stephen Shute and Susan Hurley (New York: Basic Books, 1993), pp. 135–47. Further page references will be given in the main body of my chapter.

16. In the last chapter of *The Future of the Image*, Rancière argues that the paradox of Lyotard's sublime is that it seeks to disrupt the machinery of dialectical thought by drawing on the conceptual resources of its philosophical 'master': 'In short, the concept of art summoned to disrupt the Hegelian machine is none other than the Hegelian concept of the sublime' (p. 133). Whether or not this is true, Rancière rereads Hegel to argue that, for the latter, the sublime does not simply entail a symbolic art that cannot find an adequate material form for its idea, and which is therefore prior to representation; more complexly, with the decline of representative art and the Romantic separation of form and content, the sublime makes possible 'a new symbolic moment' which is (at) the *end* of art, one that insists through a strongly polemical gesture on Hegel's part that after 'the dissolution of the determinate relationship between idea and material presentation' (p. 136), as Rancière puts it, art is simply over, once and for all. For Rancière, Lyotard's disastrous move is therefore to reappropriate this 'end' in terms of an interminable (ethical) debt to the 'Other'.

17. For a more detailed exposition of Rancière's thought on this topic, see the final chapter of *The Future of the Image* entitled 'Are Some Things Unrepresentable?' which as noted above includes some further critical remarks in a similar vein directed at Lyotard. In closing, Rancière affirms that, to the extent that it removes limits placed on the possibilities of representation, the 'maladjustment' involved in an art which breaks free from the representative form 'tends towards more representation, not less' (p. 137). Meanwhile, the logic of the 'unpresentable' is deemed 'vacuous' in the sense that it wants to abolish representation by severing forever the link between 'forms' and 'subjects' while at the same time clinging desperately (Rancière says, terroristically) to the notion of certain forms that permit such an (ethical) achievement to be measured.

18. See note 8 above.

19. Lyotard therefore continues: 'The likeness that they have in common follows from the difference of each from each' (p. 136).

20. Rancière, *The Ignorant Schoolmaster: Five Lessons in Intellectual Emancipation*, trans. Kristin Ross (Stanford: Stanford University Press, 1991). The premise of this book is that the scene of teaching is characterised by an equal intelligence shared by teacher and student alike and thus that the beginnings of education are to be found in such 'equality'.

21. See Bill Readings, *Introducing Lyotard: Art and Politics* (London: Routledge, 1991), p. 86. The relationship between ethics, politics, aesthetics and law is a complicated one throughout Lyotard's thought. A good starting place for the reader interested in this complexity is perhaps *Peregrinations: Law, Form, Event* (New York: Columbia University Press, 1988). Here, via his reading of Kant, Lyotard argues that if the aesthetic community establishes 'the horizon of an expected consensus', this consensus is bound to be 'allusive and elusive, endowed with a special way of being alive, both life and death', or in other words always 'in the process of doing *and* undoing itself' (p. 38).

22. Jean-François Lyotard, *The Inhuman*, trans. Geoffrey Bennington and Rachel Bowlby (Cambridge: Polity, 1993); *Heidegger and 'the jews'*, trans. Andreas Michel and Mark Roberts (Minneapolis: University of Minnesota

Press, 1990). Further page references to the latter text will be included in the main body of my chapter.

23. See Readings, *Introducing Lyotard*, p. xxxii.

24. To my mind, Readings gives a much better translation of this passage, as follows: 'What really preoccupies us, whether historians or non-historians, is this past which is not over, which doesn't haunt the present in the sense that it is lacking, missing. It neither occupies the present as a solid reality nor haunts the present in the sense that it might indicate itself even as an absence, a spectre. This 'past' is not an object of memory in the sense of something which may have been forgotten and must be remembered (in the interests of 'happy endings' and good understanding).' (See Readings, *Introducing Lyotard*, p. 62.)

25. See Lyotard's response to Augustin Nancy, dated 5 January 1985, in Lyotard's *The Postmodern Explained to Children: Correspondence 1982–85* (London: Turnaround/Power Institute of Fine Art, 1992), pp. 81–6.

26. See Chapter Two of *Rancière's Dissensus: On Politics and Aesthetics*, 'Does Democracy Mean Something?' (pp. 45–61).

27. Fittingly, if ironically, the term is also used by Lyotard (even if its meaning is not identical with that of Rancière), for instance at the very close of *Peregrinations: Law, Form, Event*, where Lyotard writes that 'the only consensus' we should concern ourselves with pursuing is 'one that would encourage . . . heterogeneity or "dissensus"' (p. 45).

Chapter 3

Distress II

Masochistic Education

But who is this 'Other' who, whether cruelly or not, announces what they may not know? And who is the distressed *infantia* found, if Lyotard is to be believed, at the origin of the possibility of civil life? What is the nature of their pain, a pain at once inflicted and endured? Why submit to it, why silently succumb, without yet being able to attest to the reason why? From the perspective of the Deleuzian interpretation of masochism, it would be impermissible to view this quasi-self-induced distress of the child of civil education and address – this impossible and impossibly painful affirmation – as simply that of a masochist who is also a sadist in waiting. I venture this allusion to Deleuze's writing on Sade and Masoch not simply to license a somewhat arbitrary segue from one discourse to another, but to explore the possibility of some perhaps more deep-seated connections between the economy and practice of masochism outlined by Deleuze and the formation of civil life described by Lyotard. In particular, I want to show that some of the principal features and effects of what Deleuze sees as masochism's desire to educate the other correspond significantly with those of the Lyotardian 'Other' as master-teacher, and furthermore that through this comparison we might be able to complicate overly clear-cut distinctions between the 'distressing' instruction of such an 'Other', on the one hand, and, on the other, the emancipatory teaching of the ignorant schoolmaster à la Rancière. In fact, as I hope to show, it may be that the master-teacher who for Lyotard forms a couple with the distressed *infantia* at the origin of civil life is much less the 'knowing', forceful stultifier at the centre of the explicatory tradition condemned by Rancière, than they are potentially transformative educator working complexly at the (not necessarily self-identical) edges of what both masochism and emancipation might mean and do.

Let's begin with a brief summary of some of the main lines of Deleuze's thinking on masochism. In his essay 'Coldness and Cruelty', Deleuze is concerned to refute the idea, found in parts of Freud's work (and elsewhere), that sadism and masochism are just two sides of the same coin, forming a complementary or interchangeable pair, hence constituting a reversible opposition.[1] Thus, for instance, Deleuze deems stupid the old joke in which the masochist says 'hit me', and the sadist says 'no'. For Deleuze, no sadistic gratification would be obtained from willing or pleasurable suffering – 'a genuine sadist could never tolerate a masochistic victim', he insists (p. 40) – while the masochist prefers not the truly sadistic torturer, but instead a 'nature' that has been carefully moulded by masochistic wants or needs. From Deleuze's point of view, then, the term sado-masochism is largely a misnomer (as it would be, for instance, to describe the civil world), since sadism and masochism entail entirely different 'situations' in which the appearance of, say, sadistic behaviour in scenes of masochistic desire amounts less to sadism proper than to a function or expression of masochistic drives, relations and practices which, he argues, formulate themselves quite differently than is the case in the economy of sadism. Accordingly, at the end of his text, Deleuze draws up a list of key attributes that distinguish rather than align sadism and masochism (we will unpack these a little more as we go along): sadism is institutional, masochism contractual; sadism is demonstrative, masochism imaginative; there is a world of difference between sadistic 'apathy' and masochistic 'coldness'; 'sadism negates the mother and inflates the father, masochism disavows the mother and abolishes the father'; whereas sadism 'operates by means of quantitative reiteration' so as to enumerate cumulative repetitions of its violence, masochism works 'by means of qualitative suspense', taking delicious pleasure in the wait; as such, the 'aesthetic and dramatic suspense' of Masoch contrasts sharply with the sadist's total hostility to 'the aesthetic attitude' and so on (p. 134). Within this series of 'specific symptoms' attributed to sadism and masochism respectively, Deleuze draws a distinction between the sadistic instructor and the masochistic educator. While the libertine dispenses oppressive theoretical demonstrations of sadistic reason with no dialectical dimension or dialogic function, no pedagogic intention other than to establish that his reasoning is the same, cruelly overpowering thing as his violence, the masochist – far from being the passive victim of a sadistic torturer – in fact seeks through complex and subtle means to educate his tormentor, such that the latter will participate as wished in the practice and economy of masochistic desire. The role of educator constitutes itself through the masochistic 'pact': while for Deleuze the sadist is in need of institutions which overpower civil law in the interests of a state of permanent unrest, wanton anarchy and unbridled immorality, the masochist operates on the strength of contracted alliances which depend not on forms of diabolical 'possession' but upon a more or less 'civilized' compact with the other. Thus the masochist seeks to persuade. Nonetheless, his role is not to instil a credo, to convey a knowledge or even to teach a method. While the masochist's pleasure (and pain) rests upon the performance of quite rigidly defined characteristics on the other's part, which take hold as the result of a certain seduction that only the masochist is capable of, nonetheless his discourse is prescriptively 'weak', as it were – not least in the sense that it liberates as much as enchains the torturer. The letter received by the masochist protagonist of *Venus in Furs* at the very end of the novel, written by his erstwhile tormentor, is penned by a comparatively free soul (albeit that such freedom is obviously a complicated thing). Having broken away from the stifling attentions of her victim, Wanda declares that it was precisely his former enslavement to her that prohibited matrimonial ties, making them seem repulsive despite all her passionate feelings, that she had indulged him, not because of her subordination, but for her own pleasure and amusement, and to 'cure' or educate him in turn, and that her subsequent bondage to another, stronger man (soon to be killed in a duel) was inevitably short-lived given life's inevitable insecurities (in other words, that life's ties are always transitory). This is the discourse of one who – like the protagonist himself at the end (or, rather, the beginning) of the novel – has learnt the lesson of masochism only in the sense of discovering a certain freedom from it, in at least a multiple sense.

The training offered by the masochist is therefore not of the order of explication, nor does it follow from an explicative conception of the world. It neither imparts nor defends some authoritative wisdom or learning, and its relations of desire are not reducible to a (perhaps sadistic) model of instruction invested in the structural inequality of teacher as superior and pupil as inferior party. What it practices, what it does, is far more complex, dynamic, transformative and strange than any maintenance of the status quo through the elevation and reproduction of a set content or body of knowledge. If, as Deleuze suggests, the language of Sade is contradictory in effect, since 'in the gathering momentum of repetition' it 'tends to force us onto the side of the torturer' (p. 34) while still, as Bataille knew only too well, reverberating with that of the victim ('Only the victim can describe torture; the torturer necessarily uses the hypocritical language of established order and power', writes Deleuze (p. 17)), masochism offers an alternative version of the paradox, the masochist speaking the language of self-torture as guilty victim only in order to license the pleasurable subversions and strange schemes he will invent for himself. Indeed, as Masoch's novel repeatedly shows, this is the ruse that the masochist has learnt (and perhaps it is all he has learnt). To the extent that the masochist economy is an educative one, the seductive result of a certain training, it is also deceptively freeing, indeed in the very midst of suffering. In place of fixed schemas of pedagogic superiority and schoolmasterly oppression it is the cruel master or, rather, *mistress* who receives liberatory training from the subordinate, and it is the distress of the infantilised or belittled one that offers some degree of emancipatory possibility. Thus the masochist's world is not a world in which the logic or spectacle of victimhood remains reducible to the simple alternatives of servitude or freedom in relation to the master. Instead, masochistic distress frees master – *mistress* – and victim alike.

At certain points, Deleuze writes of the non-communication between sadism and masochism in terms of their mutual yet wholly distinct radical specificity, their shared yet unshareable self-enclosure. Yet if there is 'no possibility of communication between them, either from inside or from outside', as Deleuze insists, this is related to the fact that: 'Only the normal "communicate" – more or less' (p. 45). Without this 'more or less', one might be tempted to think – in contrast to that which forms their 'outside' (i.e. 'normality') – that masochism and sadism share at least one similarity, in that as an 'economy' or 'order' each expresses itself non-communicatively, as it were, let's say in the ultra-demonstrative language of the sadist rather than the dialectical-imaginative discourse of Masoch. We might even be tempted to think that such a similarity (re-)groups masochism and sadism in terms of the differend that they unshareably share. And yet to the extent that the 'more or less' of 'normal' communication suggests an irreducible supplement of otherness – that is, of non-communicability – which may perhaps accompany its very conditions of possibility, the supposedly firm, non-porous boundary between the normal and the perverse gets put into question from the outset. So that we must think again. Just as sadism perhaps unwittingly reverberates with the language of the victim that its ultra-demonstrative discourse neither recognises nor entertains, so masochism distinguishes itself as a radically specific economy (distinct from that of sadism) in the very sense that it combines communication and non-communication, the shared and unshareable, in a distinctive – and distinctly unassimilable – way. In other words, masochism is not just outside 'normal' life, whatever that may be (more or less), but might contaminate it, open on to it, in curious and perhaps not altogether negative ways. As I am suggesting, one way to conceive of this might be through thinking about the *distress* of civil life in terms of the concrete potentialities of freedom amid seemingly intractable suffering.

It Is Not a Child But a Father That Is Being Beaten

If twice now I have stressed how the master is replaced by the *mistress* in the practice and economy of masochism, this is not just for mildly comic or weakly political effect. Deleuze is quick to dispute the assumption, broadly aligned with psychoanalysis, that 'since the father-image is a determinant in sadism, this must also be true for masochism' (p. 57), the latter being from this point of view merely a reversal or inversion of the former. In such a reading, the masochistic variant of the supposedly universal desire to usurp the father entails the onset of guilt, which causes the masochist to 'renounce the active aim and take the place of the mother in soliciting the father's love' (p. 57). He wishes to be beaten to prevent further guilty feelings, the beating itself representing both a lesser form of punishment than he is really due, and a substitute for the expression of fatherly love he so craves to assuage the guilt. Why, then, does he wish to be beaten by a woman, by the mother rather than the father? As Deleuze suggests, a number of reasons are given for this, including displacement of otherwise blatant homosexual overtones, a wish to revert to the Oedipal situation whereby the punishment due from the father is re-tied to the child's identification of the mother as object of desire, and finally the attempt to substitute for the son's violent wishes those of the now-violent mother ('daddy, it's not me that wants to hurt you, look how rough she is').

For Deleuze, this is a dire misreading of what is at stake in masochistic beating. While the sadist dreams of destroying the family by entering into a sodomitic union with the daughter and inciting her to torture and kill the mother, it is nonetheless a mistake to see the father-figure behind the beatings dreamt of by the masochist. Instead, for Deleuze, far from the father being ultimately responsible for the beating handed out to her offspring by the mother, it is the father-image *within* the child himself that is asking to be beaten.[2] Despite Deleuze's contention that the two interpretations are wholly opposed, however, there is perhaps something in the psychoanalytic discovery of the child's desire to communicate to his father the violence of the mother – 'daddy, look how rough she is' – that corresponds to this acknowledgement that the one who is being beaten is in fact the father-in-the child. For 'daddy, look how rough she is' is not just a projection of guilt or an appeal for solidarity; it is perhaps also a tip-off. Be that as it may, for Deleuze the masochist wishes for the father, the father within himself, to be hurt and humiliated. Once more, Deleuze draws a sharp line between sadistic masculine power and masochistic desire, albeit one which might falter a little if we were indeed to concede that soliciting maternal violence on the child's part might also be a way of alerting the father to his 'own' beating, enacted upon the son. For Deleuze, however, the two economies do not correspond to one another, in the sense that he sees no identification with the father on the masochist's part. Instead, Deleuze suggests, what the masochist really wants is for the mother to take over the functions of the father – notably, 'the administration of cruelty' (p. 62) – rather than be destroyed by them, and all in the interests of a new contract with her child. In masochistic fantasies, she is thereby liberated from the father and so free to pursue other men (in fact, the contract obliges this) while still being empowered to beat and torture the father-in-the-son, as it were. Thus there is an attempt to cancel out the father, twice over, in the world of the masochist. From this perspective, to assume what I have begun to describe as the masochistic 'distress' of entry into civil life also makes possible new openings on to the transformative resource of a mother-figure capable of banishing a father, a sadistic patriarch who is also the most extreme threat to forms of familial and social reproduction. And it is the contract itself, as Deleuze notes, which is precisely what limits the aggressive return of the father, whether in overt or clandestine form. Its terms and conditions, closely governing all forms of behaviour and interaction between the two parties, is part of a subtle strategy to prevent such a return. In other words, if in Deleuze's terms the masochist's pact cements an alliance between son and mother to the detriment of fatherly power and to the benefit of the child's inventions, as distinct from the diabolical deal done between sadistic father and daughter in the interests of an ultra-self-destructive patriarchy hell bent on obliterating its own law, then to interpret Lyotardian civil life as something like a masochist's charter or at least mandate might join a certain gender politics onto its always potentially transformative possibility (although I suspect the chance that the masochist's pain might always tip-off the father would appeal to Lyotard's sense of the ineliminable fragility of the civil contract, and the need for ceaseless vigilance in this regard).

No doubt, Rancière would be persuaded by none of this. Doubtless he would point to Deleuze's own characterisation of masochism as an art of suspense, a state of waiting in its purest form, in order to dismiss such thinking as just another version of poststructuralism's morose sophistry, its archly elevated elaborations and refined vacillation, standing in the way of full emancipatory possibility just as much as explicatory pedagogy had ever done. He would no doubt point out masochism's tendency towards the law (as the always prospective fate of the contract), which Deleuze contrasts with the sadist's antipathy towards the law in all its forms.[3] Of course, if Deleuze is to be believed, a certain name can be given to the one person a masochist can't persuade.

Announcement

How, then, does the instruction offered by the Lyotardian 'Other' relate to that of the ignorant schoolmaster favoured by Rancière? For Rancière, the explicatory model of pedagogy, far from being responsible for liberating hitherto untutored and thus unenlightened minds, has operated historically to set a limit on education's emancipatory possibility, stultifying through an ultimately oppressive vanguardism the true learning that is grounded in the principle of freedom. Thus, in *The Ignorant Schoolmaster*,[4] he writes the following about the exiled schoolteacher Jacotot's method for liberatory 'universal teaching' during the years of Restoration in France:

> Explication is not necessary to remedy an incapacity to understand. On the contrary, that very incapacity provides the structuring fiction of the explicative conception of the world. It is the explicator who needs the incapable and not the other way around; it is he who constitutes the incapable as such. (p. 6)

If the long-standing practice and tradition of explication preserves inequality, the translator of the English edition of Rancière's *The Ignorant Schoolmaster*, Kristin Ross, asks: 'What would it mean to make equality a *presupposition* rather than a goal, a *practice* rather than a reward situated firmly in some distant future so as to all the better explain its present infeasibility' (p. xix). While such questions would seem to cut to the heart of the difference between the radically dissymmetrical scene of teaching in Lyotard and the commitment to equality in continual action in Rancière, still one might usefully repeat the question rather than just succumb to its rhetorical force. Exactly what might equality look like in practice? Here, we should recall Rancière's own insistence on the intractable role of the master in Jacotot's emancipatory method. For while in terms of free learning a traditionally masterful explicator may produce nothing but unwanted pedagogic effects, the master *is* still needed to direct the will, although not the intelligence, of the student seeking their freedom. Indeed, it is this specific interaction – that of an intelligence solely obeying its own principle while the 'will' of such an intelligent being follows and submits totally to another – that for

Rancière produces the conditions of possible emancipation. Thus, while in Jacotot's pedagogic schema the 'good' master is the one who 'teaches that he has nothing to teach', who does not place himself in the vanguard of a knowledge as such, nevertheless in order to unleash liberation in the other such a teacher's own emancipated will *must* be master. By his own example – that is, of a sheer exercise of will not governed by explicatory content or discipline – the master announces the fundamental potential of the other, without constraining the possible meaning or trajectory of that potential. As Rancière himself writes: 'This was not a method for instructing the people; it was a benefit announced to the poor . . . It sufficed only to *announce* it' (p. 18). Such announcement, as a form of discourse that exceeds and confounds explication, seems not wholly distinct from the negation of 'interlocutory expectation' that in Lyotard accompanies the Other's announcement of the right to speak. For the latter is an estranging instruction which no more sets the other's expectation of what they will come to learn or say than it ties the teacher to 'repetition and the conservation of existing meanings', to quote Lyotard's 1993 Amnesty lecture once more (p. 143). It is, in other terms, a form of self-overcoming on both sides, to borrow Rancière's own terminology (p. 42). While the emancipatory master of Rancière's book 'demands speech' as 'the manifestation of an intelligence that wasn't aware of itself or that had given up' (p. 29), Lyotard's Other commands *without* commanding speech in the specific sense that his announcement issues from a groundless ground, having no prior orientation, no self-identity, no set message, method, meaning or manifesto which would found its possibility (not even so much as 'I will teach you what I do not know' or 'everything is everything', à la Jacotot). Such speech as that of the Lyotardian 'Other' does not, therefore, homogenise or consensualise populations under a single banner or slogan, but connects people through mutual estrangement or distancing as their fundamental condition. (Indeed, Rancière himself writes that people are only ever united as people, or beings of intelligence, in the sense that all are non-aggregated, '*distant* beings' (p. 58).) The estranged recipient of the Other's instruction in Lyotard is therefore not so far away from the emancipated student of Rancière, who regains his reason and speech having reserved the right to think about what he has heard, and who thereby retains the capacity to verify the other's speech through his own replies (Rancière, p. 41) – except that the verification of reason as the upshot of this Rancièrian scene of universal teaching and emancipation would perhaps, for Lyotard, set an initial constraint upon what announcement might do, in that it would seem to involve an at least partial return of 'interlocutionary expectation'.

If, time and again, Rancière associates emancipation or proof of capacity with the realisation of speech ('the human child is first of all a speaking child' (p. 11)), and continually presents freedom as a form of action that must be fully expressed and freely verified ('the artisan must speak about his works in order to be emancipated' (p. 65)), Lyotard's insight – not entirely at odds with the logic of Rancière's thinking, albeit aggravating it in terms of the latter's own antipathies – is that only through a constitutive silence or a gap in speech can speech itself can be set free. Rancière might well deride the citizen-form as an expression of inegalitarian political models or structures, yet what is to be found at the heart of Lyotard's thinking of the basis of civil life may connect to the very possibility of universal teaching as an emancipatory act of self-expression that is also one, perhaps somewhat complicatedly, of self-overcoming. It may be that Lyotard is just a little less serene than Rancière about the fragility and the risks of such self-transformation.

Žižek in Pain

Rather like Rancière, Žižek wishes to open a pathway out of what he sees as the depoliticizing constraints of ethical thought, towards emancipatory or revolutionary possibility. He wishes to oppose what he sees as poststructuralist conceptions of difference oriented towards a certain hypothesis of the other (the shorthand for which might be 'respect for the other'), replacing them instead with an idea of difference that, for him, makes possible radically egalitarian unification through a collective politics that mistrusts diversity and spurns pluralism (in other words, communism). Interestingly, however, while one senses Rancière's utter revulsion for Lyotardian evocations of pain, Žižek's political project is often articulated precisely in terms of the radical value of pain. (One might speculate that this divergence between the two, whereby the origin and the obstacle to emancipation are given practically the same name, is itself potentially rather painful for the emancipatory project of recent theory.) Rethought against the ethical context in Žižek, this pain – of little interest to Rancière – acquires a specific theologico-political resonance.

In *The Fragile Absolute: Or, Why Is the Christian Legacy Worth Fighting For?*[5] Žižek argues that St Paul denounces the Judiac entanglement in a Law which, in order to maintain the vitality and originality of its tradition, brutally represses the violence at its own origin – even if this is the very nature of Judaism's fidelity to that same origin (pp. 97–8). Christianity, in contrast, arrives in confessional mode, announcing the violence of its founding event as the most intimate expression of Christian identity. These legacies leave complex after-effects. For instance, while for Žižek the deeper instincts of psychoanalysis lie not with confession (the talking cure), but rather with an acknowledgment of the traumatic origin – one that that remains irredeemable to the extent that it defies full expression – the theological contours of Pauline Christianity trace out the possibility of overcoming this traumatic law as an irreducible horizon of experience. In this, the Christian logic of redemption breaks with both the interminable inheritance of a Judaic past and Judaism's profound orientation towards an ever-deferred future, an always suspended messianic possibility. (Indeed, via his reading of Levinas in the more recently published *God in Pain*,[6] Žižek suggests that Judaism should move beyond a certain ethical commitment to the Law and instead embrace its legacy otherwise – the legacy expressed by the kibbutz movement and the early years of the state of Israel – consisting in new types of collectivity 'grounded in the "dead letter" of an uprooted Law' (p. 226).)

Žižek suggests that what is decisive about the Christian God in conceptual terms is that it implies not merely a formal or symbolic resemblance between man and deity, but a direct identity. Man and God simply become one in the figure of Christ. (In contrast, for him, the Judaic ban on images of the deity insists upon a fundamental separation between incarnate mankind and an abstract or unpresentable divinity.) Nonetheless, this most intimate identity of the God-man, embodied in Christ, also implies a fundamental schism, a splitting of the identity of God, as if the advent of God in man-like form reflects a more basic division already at work in the nature of God. (Christ is not divided between two natures, worldly and divine, but is marked by a more fundamental tear within the same entity, God, without which his very coming into being would be redundant.) It is in this sense that Christianity brings not peace but the sword: the Christian idea of God irrupts as scandalous event to the extent that it implies, as we read in *The Fragile Absolute*, the 'violent intrusion of Difference that precisely *throws the balanced circuit of the universe off the rails*' (p. 121). For Žižek, this originary capacity for violence at the perverse core of Christianity offers itself as a rupturing force against the sterile plurality of postmodern politics, tearing asunder its homogenising ethical discourse of the other. Indeed, on the basis of just this originary perversity, perpetually self-divided Christianity explodes anew into the world, rankling at both the inertia of a tolerant or ethical politics, on the one side, and the complacency of fundamentalist certainty, on the other. It seeks not to preserve and conceal the 'obscene supplement' of the law's foundation, but instead to open this 'supplement' to the transformative possibility of politics in a more proper sense. Put differently, in *God in Pain*, 'the Christian stance, at its most radical, involves precisely the suspension of the vicious cycle of Law and its transgressive desire' (p. 143)[7] – a cycle which, paradoxically, sees Judiac Law continually reinvoked in order to disavow the guilt this same cycle engenders – in favour of a new beginning, indeed one that, far from lying ahead in a time to come, has already begun. Thus, in fact, the figure or image of *God in pain*, a God divided within and against himself from the outset – one whose self-division is precisely the condition of man's existence, his very character as such – destines the Christian deity to a desperate Fall[8] in which is announced nonetheless the coming of the Holy Ghost, the advent of a community of believers fashioned in God's pained image, whose appearance is therefore replete with revolutionary possibility in the sense that they become allied to a profoundly fissuring force capable of throwing the entire world off balance. (Indeed, rather darkly in *The Puppet and the Dwarf*[9] Žižek goes so far as to argue that 'authentic revolutionary liberation' has nothing to do with the ultimate goal of establishing 'a blissfully neutral state of harmony and balance' in which freedom might be seen to reside, since its violence is authentically revolutionary precisely to the extent that it aims to upset the balance in fundamental terms (pp. 30–1). As such, Christianity establishes its revolutionary promise through 'a violent passion to introduce a Difference, a gap in the order of being' (p. 33).)

The terms of this analysis are reprised throughout Žižek's contributions to *God in Pain* (a text shared with Boris Gunjević). Here, though, the model is reproduced through a number of prisms. For instance, Žižek agrees with Kierkegaard that the core tension in Western spirituality is that which opposes Socrates as the figure of an inward 'journey of remembrance' to Christ as the embodiment of 'rebirth through the shock of the external encounter' (p. 34). Žižek understands this shocking encounter in terms of the Lacanian *objet petit a*, by means of which part of me is reflected back in external or objective form so as to alienate or displace me from myself all the more shockingly and decisively (the *objet petit a* regards me, seeing in me as 'object' something of which I was not aware). This, indeed, is the truly Christian experience – that of God as much as of the believer – one which, far from offering religious reassurance, intrudes upon, harasses and exiles 'us' from ourselves. Thus Christ's passion and his outcry against God ('Father, why have you forsaken me?') epitomise the deeply pained experience of a God who prays to himself – objectifies himself – in the form of just this *objet petit a*, giving rise to an experience which nonetheless confirms the direct identity of God and man within precisely this scenario of self-division.[10] While in these passages of the book, Žižek refers to the Judeo-Christian tradition in contrast to that of the Greek (Socrates versus Jesus), the terms of the opposition are curiously similar to those which distinguish Christian and Jew elsewhere in his work. Accordingly, by way of another allusion to Kierkegaard, it is only through a 'theologico-political suspension of the ethical' that we might break with the 'ethico-legal entanglement' (p. 36) that for Žižek characterises the postmodern zeitgeist (but also, frequently, the situation of Judaic law). Through this ethical suspension, argues Žižek, we might direct ourselves towards the emancipatory possibility that lies deep within Christianity's perverse core, as a hidden resource which is nonetheless to be reclaimed as the most proper form of political agency today.

Following Lacan's reversal of Dostoyevsky's idea that 'if God doesn't exist, everything is permissible', Žižek suggests that belief in God comes not at the price of certain moral prohibitions, but proffers the perhaps unexpected bonus of absolute freedom, since the true believer would only ever want to act according to God's interests and desires. (Indeed, while the permissive pleasures of the godless are always tinged with the melancholy expectation of ultimate curtailment in death, the 'message of Christianity,' as Žižek puts it in *The Puppet and the Dwarf*, is that of 'infinite joy beneath the deceptive surface of guilt and renunciation', namely the underlying promise of an afterlife in which one is set free (p. 48).) Nevertheless, it would appear to be the *pain* of the Christian God, for Žižek, that permits us to determine the proper possibility of such liberation in contrast to the unconstrained and immediate expressions of faith associated with the religious fundamentalist. For there is, it would seem, a world of difference between the machinic self-expression of the blind zealot and the disorienting shock of the *objet petit a* experienced by the pained Christian (indeed, God and believer alike). While the latter is the one to whom divinity is revealed in the form of an inner (or, indeed, family) crisis that is already underway,[11] the former blithely takes God as merely the name for a politico-theological project that is already coherently set (whether this is of a statist or anti-statist stripe). Indeed, since Žižek, in *God in Pain*, describes Islam as 'orphanic', arising essentially from a 'geneological desert' in which the Holy Family – in all of its trials and tribulations – ultimately has no compelling meaning (pp. 104–5), it is perhaps no wonder that he tends to associate religious-fundamentalist programmes with Islam, albeit a corrupted Islam, but Islam nonetheless. Certainly, in this sense, one could question the prejudicial assumptions underlying Žižek's religious characterisations, which as we will see are perhaps too frequently constructed on shaky foundations – and sometimes these are foundations which undermine rather than support the arguments he wants to go on to make.

In *God in Pain*, then, it is only a suffering God, a God agonised and burdened by the mortal pain in which he must share, who can be of any help to us today. He can help precisely because he is 'involved in history' and 'affected by it' (p. 157). This is a God who thereby participates in the world without any modicum of triumphalism or mastery, but rather by very dint of his 'Fall' into worldly life. In Schelling's terms, as Žižek points out, such a God is as much a 'life' as a 'being' (indeed, to identify God as such is to make some pretty hefty, if interesting, theological decisions). In fact this Christian God of Žižek's resonates with Hegelian thought to the extent that, as Peter Dews has observed, 'throughout Hegel's mature philosophy of religion . . . he emphasizes the abstract, lifeless character of a God who does not enter fully into the finitude and agony of the world . . . Christianity, Hegel declares, begins with "pain" (*Schmerz*) – the ultimate pain of the self-conscious experience of finitude, from which not even God is exempt.'[12] Thus, for Žižek, Christianity is in fact the first religion to 'demystify the Sacred' (p. 68),[13] with Christ emerging as a pure singularity into which all abstract universals are concretely swept together and obliterated, as it were (p. 180). It is, thus, this paradox of Christianity as a religion without the sacred that for Žižek gives rise to practical possibilities in the social and political world, without risking the utter lapse into moribund secularised rationalisation.[14]

Just as – to stay with in *God in Pain* – 'Christ dies on the cross not to be rid of his mortal form and rejoin the divine; he dies because he is God' (p. 181), his very self-belief defined precisely by a certain suspension of self-belief ('Father, why have you forsaken me?), so in *The Puppet and the Dwarf* it is the Christian God's impotence that provides the key to his true significance. Indeed, if in *God in Pain* we see a Christian God uniquely in revolt against himself,[15] this only reprises similar assertions found near the beginning of this earlier work. Here, the image of a God in self-revolt epitomised by the figure of Christ is reflected in that of the believer as the one who betrays. Thus Judas can be seen as a truly heroic character in the New Testament story in the sense that he is prepared to sacrifice himself absolutely in order to ensure that the Christian revolution fulfils itself. For Žižek this scene of mutual abandonment rather than fidelity that structures the relations of God, Christ and Man finds its echo in the readiness of latter-day revolutionaries to betray personal loyalties for the higher cause, so that such betrayal is the measure of commitment itself.

Beyond all of this self-inflicted rebellion against divinity, however, God's impotence must be understood in a particular sense. Christ's suffering, like that of Job before him, is shockingly meaningless. In *The Puppet and the Dwarf*, it is not 'an act of meaningful exchange' (p. 125), either between the Father and the Son or between God and Man, but is instead an expression of powerlessness that in fact unites as much as divides them. In this regard, 'Father, why have you forsaken me?' is much less the stunned, and terrifying, acknowledgment of an imperious and aloof deity than it is the shocked realisation (shared at some point by all children) that the father can do nothing. It is in this sense that, at the moment of Christ's passion, God *as God* dies – God-the-Father as much as God-the-Son.

What the passion dramatises is Christ's excruciating exclusion from the realm to which he nevertheless truly belongs. In this, he is established as the figure of a radically egalitarian universality, in the sense that he comes to embody – absolutely – the man who has no proper place or particular part in the (social) whole, and who thereby paradoxically represents its concept all the better, all the more completely. 'Lacking any specific difference', as Žižek puts it in *The Puppet and the Dwarf*, such a man as unpartitionable remnant comes to 'directly embody true universality' in the paradoxical form of an absolute difference (p. 109). (Here, just as in regard to his disdain for the ethical, Žižek's argument echoes similar ideas found in Rancière's work.) It is in the sense that nothing less than this absolute difference can establish egalitarian possibility that Žižek insists on the dying, desanctified God – in other words, God-in-pain – as the perverse origin of the revolutionary promise.

But if Judaism is divided against itself as both the obstacle to and origin[16] of Christian radicality (that is, Judaism as both the source of an inhibiting ethical commitment to the Law and a more original instantiation of the Law's rootless violence; Jews, as Žižek argues, as at once the remainder granting access to the possibility of universal humanity[17] and yet perpetually entangled in the obfuscations of messianic waiting), and if Judaism always hazards exposure to the other of itself that it barely recognises, then in what way does it not participate in the (perverse) form of Christianity understood precisely in terms of self-division and the experience of the *objet petit a*?[18] No doubt Žižek would be ready with some neat distinctions. But at the very least, surely the differentiation of Christian and Jew would then be a pained or an agonised one, as is indeed suggested by Žižek's own wavering renditions of the relationship between the two that occur at various points in his writing. And through such pained demarcation or separation, wouldn't Judaism's agonised relation to the Christian God-in-pain redouble rather than resolve itself? Perhaps even more to the point, if this complexity pertains then why insist on the radical specificity of the Christian as granting special access to revolutionary possibility? Why have confidence, as Žižek would seem to do, in formulations such as 'the passage from Judaism to Christianity' (p. 140) – which, in the part of *The Puppet and the Dwarf* from which this phrase emanates, is also the passage away from Levinas and Derrida – when such questions obviously complicate the possibility of a linear pathway through which one comes to super-sede the other? If such messianism smacks of transcendence rather than the Fall, it seems to diverge formally from just the kind of 'properly inhuman excess' which for Žižek disturbs 'self-identity' – an excess within the human, overspilling all of its borders, that he identifies with the very name of Christ (p. 143). In other words, just as Žižek's charac-terisations of Islam look to be based on some dubious assumptions of his own making, so the idea of a passageway from Judaism to Christianity (troubling enough, to many, on more common-sense grounds) would not seem to be supported by the conceptual apparatuses Žižek himself constructs in order to assign some form of identity to each of these terms. The God-in-pain thesis, in other words, rests on some pretty pained distinctions of its own.

Levinas's Brunschvicg

A very different conception of the 'Christian' and the 'Judaic', or of the resources for the future of the Abrahamic religions, may be found in Levinas's writings on Léon Brunschvicg. In 1949, four years after the end of the Second World War, Emmanuel Levinas wrote a short essay[19] in memory of Brunschvicg, who in the year before the war's ending had died an elderly man, lying low in Aix-les-Bains. From 1942 onwards, Brunschvicg had, as Levinas observes, been denied the oppor-tunity to 'take part in any activity' by the Vichy regime, although this had afforded him the chance to review the notebooks in which, since the 1890s, he had written daily diary entries, to be read by his friend Élie Halévy, the French philosopher and historian (many of them were returned to him shortly after Halévy death in 1937). Concentrating on Brunschvicg's return to these diaries, against the backdrop of both war and old age, Levinas's essay fosters the conceit of a dialogue between the elderly and youthful 'self' of a Jewish scholar whose identity and history – both personal and public – were much tied to the European idea or project. In particular, on rereading the notebooks afresh, the idealistic youth – initially strange to the older man of experience – gradually becomes more familiar as another version or representation of 'me', despite all of life's subsequent 'failures and compromises' (p. 41), as if even at this late stage in European history a prewar 'self' can not only be recalled but still identified with in some fashion.

Born in 1869, Brunschvicg was an idealist philosopher known for his studies of Descartes and Spinoza, although he is also remembered for his work on Pascal, including the standard edition in French for which he was responsible. During the interwar years, Levinas had attended Brunschvicg's courses at the Sorbonne, which, so some of Levinas's correspondence suggests, were found not to be entirely satisfactory or compelling, philosophically speaking. The subsequent connection between the two, comparatively slight though it was, probably arose from Brunschvicg's interest in Husserlian phenomenology (Brunschvicg had been instrumental in organising Husserl's lectures on the *Cartesian Mediations* at the Sorbonne). However, Brunschvicg is remembered here not just as a philosopher of the Sorbonne, but as a Jewish intellectual at the time of the Dreyfus Affair[20] who, however much he later despaired in the face of the horrors of the Second World War, must be recalled as one who fought on the side of the victors in the political scandal that divided France at the turn of the century and who also stood for the victorious side in 1918. In this, in fact, his Judaism is not singularly paramount, says Levinas (although neither can it be split decisively away from the European that he also 'is', for reasons Levinas later elaborates). As such, to remember Brunschvig is to recollect 'a whole generation' of whom it can be said that what was most important was not the possibility of injustice in a supposedly civilised age, but 'the triumph recorded by justice' itself. 'This memory marked them', insists Levinas (p. 43). More than his philosophy, it is this feature of Brunschvicg's 'life' that Levinas considers most noteworthy.

In many ways, then, the passing of a man like Brunschvicg provides the occasion for Levinas to question or complicate the synonymous idea of the passing of an age. Brunschvicg is associated with virtues and ideas that many felt must perish – indeed, had already succumbed – with the advent of two world wars. Levinas does not shy away from the image of Brunschvicg as a European Jew born in the last century who is also a man of European culture and civilisation, but instead affirms the continuing importance of those same attributes that may be recalled in his name. Without hesitation, he celebrates Brunschvicg as a man of reason and of the university, drawing connections between the scholarly disposition, the refusal of vulgar thought and the taste for justice in terms of a 'civil status' that Brunschvicg both participates in and epitomises

(p. 43). This 'civil status', remarks Levinas, came down to the fact that, through a commitment to proof rather than propaganda, men of Brunschvicg's generation had 'proved the existence of justice' (p. 43). Indeed, Brunschvicg is recommended as an example to those among the postwar 'Jewish youth' who understandably feel immense disenchantment with the whole proposition of Europe and the West (of which Levinas was also strongly critical at various points in his philosophical career[21]), and who only see a future beyond its borders, in a 'simple life on a soil that is worked and defended with self-sacrifice and heroism' (p. 39). Levinas counsels that the virtues which helped to found and secure Israel must not be presumed to consume without remainder the resources of a 'renewed Judaism'. The 'basic toughness and straightforwardness' of the farmer-soldier of the Israeli state should not be allowed to exhaust the meaning or significance of the Jewish diaspora. (In any case, our previous chapter on Ernst Jünger's ultra-reactionary warrior-workers of the interwar years in Germany might lead us to question whether the farmer-soldier type of the Israeli state is entirely a non-Western invention, or whether it is just as much a symptom as a solution in regard to the West's 'crisis'.)[22] Instead, the critical attributes of a lively and learned intelligence must survive, including the sense of irony which, through reference to Brunschvicg's own youthful reflections in his diary entries from the early 1890s, Levinas takes to complicate too-simplistic notions of the relation of thought – or faith – to action. If, in contrast to the attitudes found among young farmer-soldiers of postwar Israel, Brunschvicg's juvenilia should be regarded as born of an era of comparative peace and happiness, Levinas nevertheless salutes peace as 'man's vocation', in rather the same way that recollection of the Dreyfus Affair prompts not the memory of injury and wrongdoing so much as the happy remembrance of victory and justice. As far as this particular essay is concerned, then, the idea of peace is not absolutely blighted by the experience of unjust war,[23] any more than the appeal of justice is quelled by offences against it, however heinous they may be. On the contrary, renewal – including 'Jewish' renewal – comes as much from the memory that injustice did not prevail, as from the harsh lessons of its experience. In this respect, then, the crisis of modernity sensed in the aftermath of war cannot merely be reduced to the deficiencies and defects of prewar attitudes and ideas (which were so often referenced precisely to legitimate such a sense of crisis) since there is also something in the prewar mindset that remains of value for postwar life. Indeed, one implication of Levinas's writing on Brunschvicg is that the very nature or meaning of any such 'crisis' depends crucially upon how one responds to it now and in the future, so that from this

perspective it looks far from simply an implacable or immutable catastrophic inheritance (of the kind Rancière associates with the emergence
of the ethics-of-the-other position).

Brunschvicg was born into an age of 'material security' in which
'every revolution was already over', Levinas tells us, and in which equi-
librium therefore reigned among Europe's great powers. The ideological
meaning of nation-states such as Germany and Russia had not yet intensified in the political form witnessed in the twentieth century. The possibility of forms of self-expression and enquiry not limited to directly
'political' responses to historical and social conditions potentialised
certain types of distance or detachment in which phrases 'light but rich
in possibilities' might not simply degenerate into 'maxims', as Levinas
puts it (p. 42). This is evoked as 'civilized speech', wholly divorced from
'speechifying'. For that matter, it is for Levinas far from reducible to
merely the immediate 'concerns' of the author or speaker himself. In
other words, such speech is open, responsive, hospitable to other meanings and possibilities; it trembles with the possibility of 'thought' not
limited to merely a self-assertive or self-gratifying intention, constituting
instead a certain type of 'resistance' in language which excites thinking
(p. 42). Such resistant language is traced back by Levinas to Brunschvicg's
'French training' at the École normale supérieure – indeed 'to everything
that is most nobly French about the traditions of that School' (p. 42).
Here, as Brunschvicg himself writes in 1942, if expression 'betrays the
thought that it should have served', still thought is tasked with subduing
'the rebellious slave' that nonetheless excites it.[24] It may be, as Levinas
remarks, that this conclusion somewhat echoes the idea Brunschvicg has
in his very first notebooks of the early 1890s concerning the profound
inexpressibility of thought. If so, as a 'man' as much as a philosopher,
Brunschvicg's very 'life' may well be characterised, and perhaps dominated, by this idea of a 'thought' that cannot bring to book or place in
order the forms of self-expression it requires – though such an incapacity
is less a limitation or failing than a virtue, a strength, indeed an origin of
sorts. (It is for this very same reason, perhaps, that Levinas is unwilling
to reduce such a lifetime to mere 'biography' (p. 39). The latter would
be inadequate in the sense that the more complex relations of thought to
language recalled via Brunschvicg necessarily problematise the very conditions of biographical writing, and also therefore because on this same
basis such a lifetime cannot be reduced to a single, personal biography.
Henceforth, Brunschvicg's life cannot help but become exemplary or
indicative, in ways that Levinas deliberately puts to use throughout his
essay.) The notion of a language resistant to and yet inspiring of thought,
one that hesitates at the limits of its own self-expression (as opposed to

the idea of a more immediate and direct relation of thought or faith to action) is of course being promoted here as an inheritance that is also a necessary supplement to the attitudes of today's 'Jewish youth'. Cross-fertilised by the European and the Judaic, rather than emanating from their decisive separation, this inheritance is once more connected with a memory not just dominated by catastrophe or disaster, but enriched by possibility itself.

If, for the likes of Rancière, Levinas might represent a certain origin of the ethical position to be lamented in philosophy, one that Rancière depicts as perpetually paralysed by the sense of an oppressively trau-matic history which those who desire emancipation must escape at all costs, it is therefore important to remember the Levinas who writes 'The Diary of Léon Brunschvicg'. For in this text, we are not just trapped by the past, although neither is the future dependent upon simple flight from it. On two counts, then, this Levinas problematises Rancière's dis-course, eluding his reductive image of the 'ethical' as just a state of per-manent and inescapable mourning and at the same time weakening the premise or rationale of its emancipatory alternative – in other words, its line of flight. For Levinas, unfettered by a propagandist will-to-power Brunschvicg epitomises a desire for justice that is neither retributive, slavish nor located in what Levinas terms 'the horrible prestige of the Sacred'. Furthermore, not 'the slightest trace of a specifically Jewish reaction' can be detected in the 1942 notebook entries, writes Levinas, although Brunschvicg 'was a member of the Central Committee of the Israeli Alliance from well before the war and never tried to forget his origins.' His desire for justice is founded instead upon the 'moral con-science' that cements his 'civil status' (p. 43). Thus Levinas's Brunschvicg hardly resembles the Rancièrian subject of an ethics of the Other (although he does look something more like Lyotard's civil-human). As Levinas observes, one may well decry – and no doubt justly – the 'pro-foundly respectable form of successful assimilation' of men like Brunschvicg for whom Judaism is still a defining characteristic, but nonetheless the latter's assimilation is not to be put down to 'betrayal' but instead proceeds from 'adherence to a universal ideal' that surpasses any 'particularism'.[25] (While Levinas does not dwell upon the idea that certain forms of Jewish 'particularism' might be resistant to this 'univer-sal ideal' – a resistance that would, here, not be his own – it should also be recalled that in this essay resistance does not so much set a limit upon what it resists, but rather *excites* it.)

In a way that once again eludes Rancière's characterisation of what we might term a post-Levinasian ethical position, Brunschvicg is avow-edly non-sentimental. Mistrust of sentiment and avoidance of platitude is essential in responding with intelligence to grief. Such intelligence must resist rigid forms of thought or 'static ideas' that stifle its creativity (as having futural capacity), and in this must maintain its aptitude for irony. Levinas recalls the 1937 Descartes Congress during which 'new philosophical tendencies' such as existentialist and Marxist thought (avant-garde Catholicism, too) 'were already being affirmed' so as to address topics that were self-consciously contemporary: 'Anguish, death, care' (p. 44). One participant, Gabriel Marcel, bitterly attacked thinkers like Brunschvicg for their 'intellectualism' or lack of 'inner life', which Marcel associated in turn with a lack of care for God and death on their part. According to Levinas, Brunschvicg's bone-dry retort was that he, Léon Brunschvicg, was indeed much less preoccupied by his own death than Marcel was with his. (The fact that Levinas takes pleasure in this remark might also be linked to his concern, in the 1934 'Phenomenology' for instance, for the Heideggerian attitude towards death as the 'proper' of being, something he would connect not only with the climate of Heideggerian thought but also with the philosophy of Hitlerism.) In a flash of irony, the coldness and detachment attributed to men of Brunschvicg's stripe is refigured as a necessary bulwark against the ultimately narcissistic, self-regarding and self-gratifying hyperbole of the impassioned counterpart. Brunschvicg's 'inner life', insists Levinas, is not dominated by 'mysticism' or 'religious anxiety' of the kind that prevails upon a Christian existentialist like Marcel,[26] but proceeds from the deep-felt values of 'reason and enlightenment' (p. 44), such that any idea of God (even a Jewish God) he may have had would arise from the 'coincidence of rational activity and moral conscience' (this would therefore be the God of Descartes rather than Pascal, as Levinas himself observes). Such thinking commits itself to one immediate concern only, that of justice, which, if it is to be demanded at all – that is demanded justly – must be demanded immediately. Levinas associates such a demand, then, not with 'the mystical experiences and horrors of the Sacred' (of the type that linked 'the supposed religious revival of our contemporaries' (p. 45) to political objectives of different kinds – in other words, various forms of political ontology or theology), but instead with a type of 'atheism' (the sceptical element of which establishes the true conditions of possibility of faith, as Derrida has asserted in Levinas's wake,[27] so that such atheism can here be referenced by Levinas as bringing us 'much closer to the One God' than the theologico-political revival to which he alludes).

Levinas concludes his essay by stating that, while 'our generation could not derive from the experience of Hitler what Brunschvicg's generation derived from the Dreyfus Affair', nevertheless its experience, however traumatic, demonstrates once more the possibility of justice, although Levinas quickly asserts that he has no desire to see this demonstration repeated – in other words, he harbours no wish that history (the history of immense suffering) be replayed. Such a reaction is not just dominated by trauma. Nonetheless, history is not to be forgotten through the more direct gesture of pure flight. Levinas hopes that the 'new spiritual and sometimes geographical horizons' of 'today's Jewish youth' do not blind them to what is precious in the past. Although he does not say as much, it seems clear that such 'gold-dust' might be prized as something that may aid future resistance against the repetition of an otherwise disregarded history. (As such, the past is to be remembered not only so as to endlessly preserve or reprise trauma, but also to resource a difficult freedom, to protectively equip it against any recurrence of the horrors from which it emerged.)

In another essay by Levinas from the same period, published just two years later in 1951, Brunschvicg crops up once more. 'Being a Westerner'[28] starts out by acknowledging the widespread sense of loss and despair at the end of two world wars, whereby faith in reason, science, progress and 'human dignity' seem to have given way to thanatology, new forms of mysticism, the will to power and a taste for the irrational. However, Levinas speculates that reason's fall from grace has less to do with the twentieth century's 'moments of anguish and ecstasy' (the test of which one might presume it had failed) than with its withdrawal into itself 'by virtue of its very nobility' (p. 46). In other words, Levinas seems to imply, it is a mistake to see in the aftermath of two such terrible wars proof of reason's innate shortcomings; if anything, such crises attest to a need for reason to be newly mobilised. If Léon Brunschvicg's name may be associated with a sense of the 'absolute society' or enclosed tradition of reason – 'Galileo, Descartes, Kepler, Huyghens, Newton, Cantor, Einstein' – the intellectual output of which is considered by him to be coterminous with its best moral and religious sensibilities, nevertheless for Levinas Brunschvicg's work continues to speak to us from beyond the grave, with, it is hoped:

> the salutary effect of giving a bad intellectual conscience to those who have forgotten, using the pretext of youth, what has after all, for three centuries, now gauged the exact gap between thought and childishness. (p. 46)

Brunschvicg's example demonstrates what must not be forgotten, namely reason's call, the irreducibility of an address to the other that forms the indispensable supplement of its inner consistency. Reason must therefore open itself to the other of itself, in this case stirring in those who languish and revel in their 'childishness' the 'bad intellectual conscience' of which they are guilty. If for Lyotard the distress of the *infantia* represents the very condition of possibility of civil locution and society, in Levinas we find the sense (which one may indeed refract out of a certain Lyotard) that such infantile experience obtains its true meaning and significance only through the passage to adulthood: that is, in the proper acquisition of what Levinas terms 'civil status' (albeit, for Lyotard, such 'status' is always marked by a certain divisibility, rendered other-than-itself by the 'right' or demand of speech, thus being shared unstably with the 'other' that one also always 'is'). In this respect, it is interesting that another lecture included in *Difficult Freedom*, where the two texts under discussion are collected (along with other essays on Judaism), was given the title 'A Religion for Adults'.[29] Here, in a way that is reminiscent of the discourse of 'Being a Westerner', Judaism is assigned the avowedly educative task of decharming the world, as Levinas puts it, 'contesting the notion that religions apparently evolved out of enthusiasm and the Sacred' (p. 14). (We might note the stark contrast with Žižek's claim that it is Christianity, rather than Judaism, which demystifies the Sacred.) This is in the interests of 'freedom', in Levinas's terms ('freedom' being equated here with 'conscience'[30]). Judaism is for adults in the sense that in Judaism one must attain the 'age of doubt', as Levinas puts it, in order to resist false pieties. Indeed, it is this that ties Judaism to the West, since the 'Western spirit', or 'philosophy' in other terms, is perhaps 'in the last analysis the position of a humanity that accepts the risk of atheism' (p. 16).[31] As the essay proceeds, this position – one of a godly atheism, one might say, or of spiritual conscience – is linked by Levinas to the possibility of ethics and justice. It is in this context that Levinas speaks of the Other. But the 'freedom' to which Levinas alludes, and to which much of his philosophical career demonstrated powerful commitment (over and above, for instance, the binding sense of past and destiny he elsewhere associates with the pagan concept of fate that helps define Hitlerian 'particularism'[32]) is 'not in the least bit pathological, or strained or heartrending'. It 'relegates the values to do with roots and institutes other forms of fidelity and responsibility. Man, after all, is not a tree' – 'freer forms' are required if 'all those heavy and sedentary things' ('the dark voices of heredity' or the call of the 'village') are to be surpassed in the interests of precisely those 'other forms of fidelity and responsibility', and, in particular, in favour of 'a freedom with regard to history in the name of morality' (pp. 22–3). (All of this, one might note, seems quite at odds with Rancière's characterisation of the emergence of an ethics-of-the-other position in terms of some paralysing sense of obligation and retrogression.)

In 'Being a Westerner', then, Brunschvicg's books are celebrated as bulwarks against voguish irrationalism, primitivism, mysticism or (as Levinas puts it) 'mythology and war', and against the widespread rumour of a 'crisis of the scientific spirit' (acknowledged as symptomatic by Leo Strauss in his lecture on postwar German philosophy, in which, as we saw previously, Jünger was held up as a telling example). In fact, his books are presented as a (pedagogic) instrument with which to curtail such adolescent behaviour and thus facilitate the onset of maturity (pp. 47–8). Just as 'thought' must strive to master the 'rebellious' language that excites it, so we might say that the 'childishness' which reason must curtail is also that which asks of its inner consistency that it speak to the other. (If I am attempting a partial synthesis here of thinkers as different as Lyotard and Levinas, it is in the interests of reinforcing my general point that these figures of an ethics-of-the-other, to recall Rancière's discourse, do not just promote perpetual retrogression or mourning of loss, but instead encourage futural thinking about 'civil status', let's say, in which the idea of the 'other' as revered primordial origin must be treated with some suspicion.)

In 'Being a Westerner', then, reason in general must not be static,[33] but mobile, creative, open, future-oriented, hospitable. It must explore new ideas as much as guard valuable ones. In particular, however, the 'thought' of the West (as its very 'spiritual life') differentiates itself from forms of religion based on the notion of salvation.[34] It must free itself from the desire for salvation that Levinas believes embodies a powerful form of egoism. For Brunschvicg, such 'self-love' as is witnessed in the striving for salvation implies in turn a certain detachment from God (that is to say, in Levinas's interpretation, a departure from the disinterested moral and religious values consonant with enlightenment and reason that, once stripped of theologico-political drive or will-to-power, ensure man's dignity and, as it were, his spirituality) (pp. 47–8).[35] For Levinas, Judaism has the potential resources to combat the 'childishness' of which he speaks because, in favouring 'inner morality' over 'outer dogmatism', it eschews the 'supernatural', or the 'impure element of magic and sorcery and that drunkenness of the Sacred and of war that prolong the animal within the civilized' (pp. 48–9). Whatever one might have to say, today, about the evocation of animality here, what is clear is that Levinas speaks against *not for* an entire ensemble of ideas with which Rancière suggests the ethics-of-the-other position is associated. The sacred or the mystical (or a feeling of redemptive entitlement) is no more indulged than a sense of war is oppressively retained as merely a species of traumatic repetition. Rather, these ideas are well understood to belong more properly to the opposing side, as it were (namely, to those forces that give rise to the likes of a Jünger, who as we have seen blended cultic myth with the dream of permanent warfare). For Levinas – supposedly the ethical thinker par excellence – in the wake of World War Two, and all that it stood for, such ideas are therefore to be resisted *not* embraced by Europe and Judaism alike. Brunschvicg's is 'a profound text', 'not because it involves the extrinsic witness of history, but because it denounces the very ambiguity of exaltation' (p. 49).[36]

Of course, Levinas's entire thought cannot be reduced to his writings on Brunschvicg, nor explained by them. But if his postwar writing is a work of mourning, it also envisages an ethics of the other capable of articulating itself to, not retreating from, political ontologies, as part of a philosophical project bent on 'destroying the philosophical premisses of the Nazi "Jewish Question"', as Howard Caygill has put it.[37] A philosophical project, in other words, that hoped to free us – in however difficult a sense – from its trauma, as much as to recall it. Levinas's writing after the Brunschvicg texts is far from just a philosophical working-through of these attitudes. As Caygill demonstrates, it often navigates a difficult and sometimes distressing path between the philosophical and the political, notably in relation to Levinas's somewhat agonised relationship to Israel. (At times when Levinas is more 'philosophically' critical of the state-form, the idea of citizenship is allied to the problem of assimilation, a criticism to which Lyotard's notion of civil life as expressed by the other-than-human/other human offers a possible rejoinder.) But, so close to the experience of war, what the Brunschvicg writings do suggest is that the attitudes which impelled the development of such an ethics were not merely founded upon the sense of an absolutely unsurpassable catastrophe.

Notes

1. Gilles Deleuze, 'Coldness and Cruelty', in *Masochism* (New York: Zone Books, 1991), pp. 9–138. Further page references will be given in the main body of the chapter.
2. Deleuze's phrase 'it is not a child but a father that is being beaten' alludes, of course, to Freud's famous 1919 essay, 'A Child is Being Beaten'.
3. In distinction to the masochist's preference for the contract, which risks the transition to law, the sadist seeks institutions capable of transcending the law (such as the Revolutionary institutions demanded by Saint-Just). However, Deleuze writes that, while in the economy of sadism and its practice of institutions, the law is 'subverted by the upward movement of irony to a principle that overrides it', in masochism we find 'the downward movement of humor which seeks to reduce the law to its further consequences' (p. 88) – that is, to humorously subject the law to its own extremes (not least

extracting its punishments in order to license transgression and thereby subvert guilt) so as to place in check the momentum which threatens to convert the contract into law. We might well expect that Ranciere would be unimpressed by such nuancing of the masochist contract.

4. Jacques Rancière, *The Ignorant Schoolmaster: Five Lessons in Intellectual Emancipation*, trans. Kristin Ross (Stanford: Stanford University Press, 1991). Further page references will be given in the main body of the chapter.

5. Slavoj Žižek, *The Fragile Absolute: Or, Why Is the Christian Legacy Worth Fighting For?* (London: Verso, 2009). Further page references will be given in the main body of the chapter.

6. Slavoj Žižek, *God in Pain: Inversions of Apocalypse* (with Boris Gunjević) (New York: Seven Stories Press, 2012). Further page references will be given in the main body of the chapter.

7. In *The Puppet and the Dwarf* (see note 8 below), Žižek argues that Bataille, for one, remains trapped within this self-same cycle, whereby transgression and the law become mutually dependent – a cycle that Žižek presents as simply the consequence 'of the Kantian philosophical revolution', one that pertains today in the form of capitalist consumption, among other things. The way to escape or undo this cycle, for Žižek, opens up at the point one recognises that the true or absolute 'excess' resides not in the law's transgression but in its founding possibility (p. 56). For Žižek, Christianity at its perverse core makes possible freedom from the guilt that the cycle or circle of law/transgression engenders, and it is in this sense that it is potentially revolutionary.

8. In *The Puppet and the Dwarf* Žižek says of the Fall that it is really only ever a form of Salvation that has been misrecognised as such, so that Salvation in its truest sense does not aim to reverse the Fall but instead complete it (p. 87).

9. Slavoj Žižek, *The Puppet and the Dwarf: The Perverse Core of Christianity* (Cambridge, MA and London: MIT Press, 2003). Further page references will be given in the main body of the chapter.

10. Thus in the midst of a discussion of Hegel, Kant and Kierkegaard, in *God in Pain* Žižek writes that the radical Christian experience redoubles alienation in the sense that it provides 'insight into how my alienation *from* the Absolute overlaps with the Absolute's self-alienation: I am "in" God in my very distance from him' (p. 175). A few pages on, he puts this differently: 'In Christianity, the gap that separates God from man is not effectively "sublated" in the figure of Christ as god-man . . . the gap is transposed into God himself, as the gap that separates Christ from God the Father; the properly dialectical trick here is that the very feature which appeared to separate me from God turns out to unite me with God' (p. 180).

11. This would be the 'family' crisis, in perhaps a double sense, that Christianity inherits from Judaism, but which according to Žižek Christianity seeks to transform in particular ways, not least through assuming the emancipatory possibility of the death of God, not just in terms of some project of rational secularisation, but as we will see by actively *living on through that death* in a more profound sense.

12. See Peter Dews, *The Idea of Evil* (Oxford: Blackwell, 2008), pp. 85–6.

13. In fact, as we shall see, Levinas makes a similar claim for Judaism, though with quite different consequences.

14. During his reading of Hegel in *God in Pain*, Žižek therefore suggests that Christianity in its perverse or paradoxical form as a religion without the sacred makes possible the overcoming of the Enlightenment separation of faith and reason, one in which – as Hegel saw – reason risks becoming reduced to a mere instrument of the intellect while religion dwindles into the expression of inner feelings which can no longer be actualised in the external world (pp. 172–4).

15. If such self-revolt suggests the revolutionary possibility that Žižek insists remains at the perverse core of Christianity, it also reflects powerfully upon what Žižek sees as false assumptions about today's 'atheistic' or secular society, a society which for him remains tied in precisely its supposed atheism to this paradox of Christian self-revolt. In this sense, one can only surmise that the relationship between revolutionary possibility and the postmodern zeitgeist cannot be reduced to a matter of simple opposition. Žižek does not ever really say as much, though neither does he ever really discount such an idea (he is more keen, at various points, to highlight a curious identity between 'liberal-skeptical cynicism' and 'fundamentalism' as both entailing a certain paucity of authentic belief (see, for instance, *God in Pain*, p. 191)); surely, though, the logic of his arguments necessitates a more thorough working-through of this problematic than his own rather episodic style permits?

16. I deliberately reprise these terms used earlier to contrast Žižek and Rancière – origin and obstacle – since it seems to me possible that this double characterisation of Judaism may point to a series of tensions within contemporary emancipatory thought that come to be projected elsewhere, i.e. in the direction of 'the Jews'.

17. In the last chapter of *The Puppet and the Dwarf*, Žižek argues precisely this: 'It is as such, as "out of place," that the Jews hold the place of universal humanity as such' (p. 131). Within the space of a few pages the 'Christian stance' is brought into sharp contrast with 'Jewish messianic expectation' as that which 'constrains us to a passive stance' since it is for Žižek only arrival that 'triggers activity' (p. 136).

18. This idea of Judaism as at once obstruction and origin of radical possibility is found, too, in *The Puppet and the Dwarf*. Here, indeed, it is its own obstruction. Žižek wishes to make perfectly clear his view that the 'mode in which Judaism has become almost the hegemonic ethico-spiritual attitude of today's intellectuals', based on openness to the unconditional call of the other, is not the 'natural' or most authentic form of what may be deemed Jewish spirituality. Nonetheless, the 'most precious elements of Jewish spirituality', namely the 'focus on a unique collective experience' for which the kibbutz offers a privileged model, are put in jeopardy by what Žižek terms Judaism's 'Pyrrhic "victory"' as ethical master (p. 9).

19. Emmanuel Levinas, 'The Diary of Léon Brunschvicg', in *Difficult Freedom: Essays on Judaism*, trans. Seán Hand (London: Athlone, 1990), pp. 39–45. Further page references will be given in the main body of the chapter.

20. In *Levinas and the Political* (London and New York: Routledge, 2002), Howard Caygill draws attention to the importance assumed by the Dreyfus

Affair not only in Levinas's thinking of the relationship between ethics and politics, but in terms of his broader politics as oriented towards a radical republicanism. Caygill also treats the Dreyfus Affair as the occasion to distinguish Levinas's response to its anti-Semitism in relation to that brand of Zionism that ultimately proceeded from coverage of the affair by the likes of Theodor Herzl, who propounded the need for radical Jewish separatism.

21. Taking just one subsequent text in *Difficult Freedom*, 'Place and Utopia' (pp. 99–102), for instance, Levinas shows himself more sharply critical of the Christian participation in Europe, in contrast to the achievements he discerns in the Jewish contribution to it. Here, Levinas is much more sceptical about Christian utopianism than, say, Žižek, arguing that its rejection of the world can foster otherworldly tendencies that often obstruct worldly change, or alternatively that may encourage partisan dwelling which answers what in 'A Religion for Adults' Levinas terms the sedentary call of the 'village'.

22. The connection between labour and freedom has frequently been a concern of French and leftist Hegelians, although the more famous example is of course found above the gates of the Nazi death camps. The postwar Levinas is critical of such valorisations of work, particularly in regard to Zionism, to the extent that for him they promote not creative endeavour but a sense of effort and fatigue that does not equate easily with the enjoyment of freedom and futurity. Nonetheless, Caygill asserts that, in his writings on Brunschvicg, Levinas (despite his fierce criticisms of Zionism) is concerned neither simply to oppose the European or 'assimilated' Jew to the Israeli farmer-soldier, nor to indicate a simple preference of one over the other, but instead to think through the complex resources of what it may mean to be Jewish or to reinvent Jewishness after the war, by looking at historical contributions beyond but not merely outside of the state of Israel.

23. Of course in *Totality and Infinity* and other texts Levinas shows himself to be far from naive concerning the continuing possibility of war.

24. Cited in Levinas, 'The Diary of Léon Brunschvicg', p. 42.

25. Levinas was critical both of assimilation and Zionist separatism (although his writings on the Israeli state are sometimes more critical than others); needless to say, however, he is at all times keen to avoid a biologistic or racial conception of the Judaic, and is indeed reluctant to concede any simple or fixed sense of Jewish identity or place in the world. The rejection of 'particularism', here, links to Levinas's critique of paganism, its concept of fate and its relationship to Hitlerism.

26. The specific character of Gabriel Marcel's Christian existentialism left him feeling at odds with a thinker like Sartre; like Jünger although in a rather different way, he was known for obsessing over technological dehumanisation in particular.

27. In 'A Religion for Adults', also found in *Difficult Freedom* (pp. 11–23), Levinas writes, as we shall see, of a monotheism which 'surpasses and incorporates atheism' (as much as, for Levinas, it would also oppose the paganism he associates with Hitlerism), but which 'is impossible unless you attain the age of doubt, solitude and revolt'. Thus such 'atheism is worth more than the piety bestowed on mythical gods' (p. 16).

28. In *Difficult Freedom* (pp. 46–9). Further page references will be given in the main body of the chapter.

29. In *Difficult Freedom* (pp. 11–23). Further page references will be given in the main body of the chapter.

30. Such a connection, made in the context of this particular text by Levinas, obviously does not fully exhaust his idea of freedom or do justice to its development, a much fuller and more complex account of which can be found running throughout Caygill's *Levinas and the Political*. In broad terms, Caygill offers a cogent demonstration of Levinas's philosophically hard-fought commitment to the notion of freedom, especially during the earlier part of his career (albeit that responsibility takes centre-stage over freedom later on, at any rate as the context in which freedom needs to be rethought). For Caygill Levinas's interest in freedom stems initially from the Bergsonian notion of creative spontaneity (although this was revised by the sense of a difficult freedom after the Second World War) rather than from a liberalistic identification with autonomy. But it is also a view of freedom that eschews the pagan concept of fate which may itself be used to contrast the cultic particularism of Hitlerian philosophy with the universalist resources of Western civilisation (albeit a 'particularism' that sought universal expansion for itself). Caygill shows how Levinas's concern with freedom powerfully affected his relationship with both Heideggerian and Husserlian thought. All of this may be placed in contrast to Rancière's notion of the advent of an ethics-of-the-other position as dominated by the sense of paralysing obligation, not creative, or even difficult, freedom.

31. Of course, throughout his career Levinas is also far from uncritical of the Western tradition as significantly a *philosophical* tradition when considered as a backdrop to the advent of Nazism.

32. See note 20 above.

33. To the extent that, for Levinas, the law is a bulwark against the dogmatism of the sacred or mysticism, it is funded by the 'inner life' of conscience and morality as, precisely, far from dogmatic or simply repetitive.

34. In *Levinas and the Political*, Caygill shows how Levinas's notion of a redeeming repentance, where it exists in some of his earlier writings, is not so much tied to the memory of an inescapable fate as inspired by the Bergsonian idea of creative spontaneity and absolute freedom in relation to the world (albeit one that Levinas later sought to refine from the standpoint of heteronomy). In 'Reflections on Hitlerism', however (the text on which Caygill concentrates in this regard), it is also true that enlightenment and reason seek to forfeit the drama of redemption and repentance, although this departure is also what licenses certain anti-liberal dramatic narratives of repentance and redemption that, in Caygill's terms, seek to exploit the deficit of liberal rationalism. Nonetheless, on this basis redemptive thought would be a supplement rather than merely an oppressive origin for future social forms (even, Levinas suggests, those deriving from Marxism).

35. In 'A Religion for Adults' Levinas writes: 'The way that leads to God therefore leads *ipso facto* – and not in addition – to man', and this same 'way' leads to man's 'self-education' (p. 18).

36. Brunschvicg is evoked in similar vein in other essays included in *Difficult Freedom*. For instance, in 'A Voice on Israel' (pp. 123–6), also from 1951,

he is cited as teaching us about the 'trace of wretchedness within the fervor of feelings' that are here associated with 'love' of, or in other words refusal to relinquish, war (p. 125), while in 'Exclusive Rights' (pp. 239–41) Levinas reprises Brunschvicg's motto: 'To mistrust every thing and love every man' (p. 239), which in the context we have been exploring surely reads as the veneration of conscience and morality (as not merely personal attributes) over propagandist or cultic politics.

37. See note 20 above.

Chapter 4

Pain of Debt, or,
What We Owe to Retroactivity

Graeber's First 5,000 Years of Debt

In his much-acclaimed book *Debt: The First 5,000 Years*,[1] published three years into the current global economic crisis, David Graeber identifies two 'origin stories' that largely dominate commonplace understandings concerning the invention of money and the onset of debt. The first is the myth of barter. According to an idealised view of archaic human communities, before money systems developed it was barter that predominated as the exchange-form characteristic of basic social relations. People simply swapped goods and services to the benefit of their own interests and, by extension, those of the community as a whole. However, the barter system had it limits. From the outset, it depended on a double coincidence of wants (I have what you want and vice versa). Then, as societies became more complex, it required increasingly sophisticated and often cumbersome multilateral transactions and valuations to ensure the desired distribution of an enlarged number of goods. Thus, the story goes, some consensual medium of exchange was required to simplify the process – hence the birth of money. Graeber shows how this 'origin story' of barter is largely founded on hypothetical language ('suppose you want eggs for your breakfast and have only bread . . .') and argues that ethnographers have yet to find any example, past or present, of a barter economy pure and simple. Rather, he points to the credit-based nature of most basic human economies as, anthropologically speaking, the more accurate and prevalent historical context for the development of money systems. Here, barter is merely an epiphenomenon in the story of money – a by-product of money systems, employed by people who for some reason or other cannot use currency and are unprepared to operate within the trust-based world of credit (for instance, while trading with strangers or enemies during times of conflict).

Why then is the 'origin story' of barter so widely accepted and so little questioned? How did it acquire currency? Graeber suggests that the myth was crucially important to the founding of economics as a discipline, and indeed to 'the very idea that there was something called the "economy," which operated by its own rules, separate from moral or political life, that economists could take as their field of study' (p. 27). From this perspective, then, money-based economies arose from the more basic situation of barter, the hypothesis of which rested in turn upon the idea of the 'objective' calculability of the value of goods – and thus the rational basis of the marketplace – outside of and prior to cultural influences or political pressures. Thus the three (abstract) functions of money identified by classical economics – store of value, unit of account and medium of exchange – simply built on the two most salient features of barter by adding a third element designed to enhance rather than detract from its essential workings. Graeber tells us that Adam Smith, who 'effectively brought the discipline of economics into being', had particular reasons for upholding the interpretation of money which arises from this 'origin story':

> Above all, he objected to the notion that money was the creation of government. In this, Smith was the intellectual heir of the Liberal tradition of philosophers like John Locke, who had argued that government begins in the need to protect private property and operated best when it tried to limit itself to that function. Smith expanded on the argument, insisting that property, money, and markets not only existed before political institutions but were the very foundation of human society. It followed that insofar as government should play any role in monetary affairs, it should limit itself to guaranteeing the soundness of the currency. (p. 24)

The story of barter makes possible this elemental image of a world where things are primarily the possessions of individuals, where each 'thing' as a form of property may be assigned a value that is essentially innate and rationally transactable, and where money is less an agent than a neutral medium of exchange made up of merely abstract units of measurement designed to serve the entirely felicitous interests of the marketplace. On this view, far from being an expression or function of power, the advent of money is a pure effect of the market in its 'free' form – from which it follows that state interference in the economy, if any, should restrict itself to upholding the currency's essential integrity as an apt medium of exchange (the paradox here, of course, is that within this laissez-faire model, where the government is merely an honest broker, such threats to the 'soundness' of money could only come from unregulated or rogue behaviour of just the kind that the free market is supposed to encourage).

For Graeber, then, the attempt to found economics as a scientific discipline on a par with Newtonian physics was not simply a matter of attaining academic credibility, since even more crucially it encouraged an analogy with the physical machinery of a Newtonian universe able to function by its own laws without ongoing divine interference, and the idea of a free market operating spontaneously and effectively (that is naturally and in everyone's best interests) outside of state intervention. (Of course, as Graeber recognises, the advent of Keynesian economics marks a certain departure from this type of thinking, opening up an alternative tradition that acknowledges money's connection to the state, in the sense that the latter establishes the legal grounds and manages the economic basis of modern exchange.) The difficulty of resisting Smith's legacy, Graeber tells us, is that by very dint of its pretensions to scientificity the founding myth of economics offers a single, unified view of the origins and development of money that is hard to dislodge with a more nuanced and differentiated picture, drawn largely from anthropological enquiry, of a whole variety of 'economic' habits and practices which, historically, often include 'mixed-mode' rather than discrete forms of exchange. (Although, for Graeber, such anthropological attention-to-detail is the best defence against retroactive historical interpretation.)

The other story of origins singled out by Graeber in his retelling of the history of debt is that expounded by proponents of the theory of primordial debt. This comes close to the Nietzchean idea (one we will come back to), found in the second essay of the *Genealogy of Morals*, whereby the ongoing prosperity of the community promotes an increasing sense of indebtedness to one's forebears, intensifying over time, until at last one's ancestors are elevated to the status of gods. Here, forms of sacrifice within human communities are interpreted in terms of the repayment of debts. Nevertheless, such 'gifts', construed as a kind of payment, paradoxically often lead to a heightened rather than reduced sense of debt, becoming evermore lavish in order to acknowledge (and thus reinforce) the very *extent* of the obligation. Primordial-debt theory suggests that, as history moved forward, governments were able to tax populations because they were table to appropriate the role of guardianship of universal debt. Once more, however, Graeber argues that there is insufficient anthropological evidence to support primordial-debt theory, and that it is itself a backward projection based on a notion of debt that is 'only made possible with the advent of the modern nation-state', the modern conception of society and of societal 'duty' and so on (p. 69). (In particular, since the theory of primordial debt is largely a European rather than an Anglo-American phenomenon, Graeber suggests that its 'mindset' is avowedly post-French Revolution.) Thus, turning to the *Genealogy of Morals*, Graeber reads Nietzsche as dabbling in primordial-debt theory not so much to embark upon an historical exposé of the origins of debt, but rather to see what happens when one starts out from 'ordinary bourgeois assumptions' (namely that the basis of human existence is 'economic' and that 'man' on earth is indebted man) in order to drive them 'to a place where they can only shock a bourgeois audience'. 'It's a worthy game', says Graeber, but one 'played entirely within the confines of bourgeois thought' (p. 79). Whether or not, on this same reading, Graeber does sufficient justice to Nietzsche's capacity to open history otherwise, once more his argument is that our conception of the origins of debt and money functions *retroactively*. That is to say, the 'origin' is generated retrospectively in order to address or promote the concerns of the present, rather than to uncover and understand the 'truth' of the past. (In fact, Graeber suggests that these two myths of origin intersect more closely than one might imagine, to the extent that it is only 'once we can imagine human life as a series of commercial transactions that we're capable of seeing our relation to the universe in terms of debt' (p. 75) – for sure, in terms of 'bourgeois thought', historically one would have little trouble connecting together beliefs about the 'economic' basis of life, on the one hand, and the religious sense of 'debt', on the other.)

How far, then, is *Debt: The First 5,000 Years* able to resist the retroactive interpretation that it is devoted to overturning? Throughout the book, Graeber wishes to counteract the insidious logic of debt: that which, by turning 'human sociality itself' into quantifiable obligations demanding repayment, inevitably recasts all human relations in terms of fault, sin and crime, redeemable 'only by some great cosmic transaction that will annihilate everything' (p. 387). He endeavours to do so by drawing a distinction between what he terms 'commercial' and 'human' economies. In human economies, which appear in a variety of historical settings, money acts 'primarily as a social currency, to create, maintain or sever relations between people rather than to purchase things' (p. 158). Interestingly, such economies are often founded on historic systems of credit, not barter, since the former implies 'trust-based interactions' and, by implication, some degree of communal solidarity and mutual aid. In human economies, however, what we owe is not reduced to a quantifiable debt requiring an exact remittance. Instead, in such communities, sociality itself is precisely the incalculable sum of debts which members share, debts to one another that they could not, nor would not wish to, fully repay. Here, then, debt is neither sinful nor criminal, but is instead an apt expression of the bonds of human sociality. Commercial economies, meanwhile, are based upon the brutality of the market, the construal of goods as property, the idea of the individual (or, put differently, the severing of people from the context of their human economies), and the abstract logic of equivalence in which even human beings become objects of exchange. Indeed, in commercial economies the reduction of human life to its market value becomes inevitable, as Graeber himself observes, at the point we accept that the exchange value of the object as a commodity is not inherent but merely an expression of its possible functions within the nexus of (property-based) human relations, which are really what is being bought and sold. By dint of a somewhat circular or self-reinforcing logic, then, the economic marketisation of human relations breeds an impersonality which fuels 'war, conquest and slavery', which in turn plays 'a central role in converting human economies into market ones' (since we are interested, here, in the question of the retroactive construction of historical explanation, in a moment we will look more closely at Graeber's account of how human communities are transformed into commercial ones) (p. 385). Commercial economies, whether in the Axial Age of Greece, India and China or in the Age of Great Capitalist Empires (to use Graeber's own headings) are thus characterised by 'impersonal markets, born of war, in which it was possible to treat even neighbours as if they were strangers', in turn allowing 'human life to seem like it could be reduced to a matter of means-to-end calculation' (p. 238). Here, the criminalisation of unrepaid debt amounts to nothing less than 'the criminalization of the very basis of society' as exemplified by human economies (p. 334).

But how exactly does 'human' economy give way to the market, if not by a circular process through which the violence inherent *theoretically* in the logic of the market creates its own *historical* conditions of possibility? Looking back over his enormous survey, Graeber describes 'how all this can begin to break down: how humans can become objects of exchange: first, perhaps, women given in marriage; ultimately, slaves captured in war' (p. 208). Surely, though, the matrimonial exchange of women is a near universal characteristic of human societies, whether 'commercial' or 'human'? (Graeber's own anthropological range offers little against this truism.) And if this is so, then it points to something more fundamental about so-called human communities, notably that they contain in themselves the basis for more or less violent forms of exchange. Such dealings are here restricted to the 'origin story' of the trading of women, but surely such exchange depends on the prior existence of some broader sense of market 'value', which is said by Graeber to arise principally with the collapse of human economies and the onset of commercial ones. The transition made by Graeber, from the trafficking or dealing of 'women' to the creation of 'slaves', implies an intensifying or worsening onset of market conditions that would only be convincing as a historical narrative if the exchange of women in matrimony were not already fundamentally a type of 'slavery'. (What makes this moment all the more odd, and indeed telling, is that throughout his survey Graeber is extremely sensitive to the historic plight of women.) And this fundamental truth disturbs and disrupts the narrative of historical transition from 'human' to 'market' economy Graeber wants to offer in place of the 'origin stories' of barter or primordial debt.

What is more fundamentally at issue here is that double and competing conceptions of money vie for primacy throughout Graeber's book. On the one hand, and more *theoretically*, money is construed as the product of an abstract conception of equivalence introduced into notions of obligation and worth. This is precisely where its violence – a violence born of deep impersonality – comes from. On the other hand, and more *historically*, however, it is viewed (contra Adam Smith) as far from a neutral medium of exchange produced by market conditions outside of state interference. Instead, in example after example, it is portrayed as nothing less than an instrument of power. (In particular, Graeber shows how the politics of taxation have served in modern times to indebt populations to their governments, destroying locally based credit systems and at the same time funding the war machines of the powerful: what he terms a 'military-coinage-slavery complex'.) This is where its violence – a violence that is, precisely, *motivated* – comes from. In the one account, then, the violence which accompanies money systems occurs as the expression of particular *interests*, while, in the other, the violence which money unleashes happens precisely because it is, to the contrary, *unmotivated* as such.

While there are moments in the book where attempts are made to resolve such difficulties, there are also instances that suggest the problem remains a persistent one. For example, in order to clarify his thesis, Graeber writes:

> The story of the origins of capitalism . . . is not the story of the gradual destruction of traditional communities by the impersonal power of the market. It is, rather, the story of how an economy of credit was converted into an economy of interest; of the gradual transformation of moral networks by the intrusion of the impersonal – and often vindictive – power of the state. (p. 332)

This 'gradual destruction' transforms the 'very essence of sociality' into the grounds for 'a war of all against all' (p. 335). Here, Graeber underscores his point that 'human economies' do, precisely, operate in terms of economic rather than non-economic practices. As he repeatedly asserts, they are credit-based as the very basis for their social systems. Thus he is able to suggest that the 'commercial' economics of interest and of the market arise on the strength of a certain mutation or perversion of what grounds human 'society' or community in the first place. From this, it seems possible to align more consistently the fundamental logic that gives rise to money with the historical emergence of modern forms of power. Nevertheless, within just a few pages, Graeber proposes the following thesis concerning the specificity of capitalism itself:

> This would seem to mark the difference. In the Axial Age, money was a tool of empire . . . money always remained a political instrument. This is why when empires collapsed and armies were demobilized, the whole apparatus could simply melt away. Under the newly emerging capitalist economy, the logic of money was granted autonomy: political and military power were then gradually reorganized around it. True, this was a financial logic that could never have existed without states and armies behind it in the first place. (pp. 320–1)

Now, there is something about this assertion that seems counter-intuitive. In terms of some aspects of Graeber's own argument, one might expect to be told, since there is something originary or fundamental about the 'internal' or intrinsic logic of money, that forms and practices of power shaped themselves around it from the very beginning. (Even if money as defined by the structural element of abstract equivalence developed subsequently to systems of credit, the latter contained the germ of what money is, namely an IOU.) But Graeber tells the story the other way around. Where once money was in its more rudimentary form a sheer political instrument, it is only subsequently (with the onset of capitalism 'proper') that money's own logic comes to the fore, remaking in its own image the political world around it. No doubt Graeber has good anthropological reasons to put this case. But the contention also smacks of the desire to resist what he sees as the foundational idea of disciplinary economics concerning the creation of a spontaneous free market prior to political or state intervention. Here, then, for Graeber, it is almost as if power comes first and money second as an epiphenomenon of power. ('True, this was a financial logic that could never have existed without states and armies behind it in the first place.') But such a suggestion threatens to undermine what would otherwise seem the highly plausible headline claim of the book (most cogently put, as we just saw, only a few pages later): namely, that it is the very basis of human sociality – *credit* – which holds the key to explaining how modern forms of politics and power arise (albeit by means of terrible mutation). One cannot help wondering whether Graeber's double and divided narrative of historical origins and development is just as retro-active as the 'origin stories' he wishes to oppose, in the sense that the tensions and contradictions I have pointed out are as much to do with unresolved theoretical questions striking at the heart of his own thesis as they are to do with the historical or anthropological complexities to which Graeber frequently refers in order to wriggle free from the sup-posed demands of a 'simple' or 'single' story that he projects in terms of the reductive figure of disciplinary economics.

Lazzarato's Indebted Man

How might one account for this seemingly intractable retroactive impulse, where the question of debt is concerned? And what are the risks of thinking, too hastily, that it can be overcome? Let's turn to another of the many recent writings on the debt crisis currently receiving a great deal of interest, Maurizio Lazzarato's *The Making of the Indebted Man: An Essay on the Neoliberal Condition*.[2] Lazzarato shows how, since the energy crisis of the late 1970s, the transformation of the way in which national expenditure on welfare is financed has resulted in continually rising national deficits. For Lazzarato, far from an unwanted or unfore-seen consequence of neoliberal policies, such indebtedness has been their ultimate aim. The intensifying privatisation of national debt linked to the ever increasing dependency of governments upon market finance and securitised credit (debt repackaged and resold in terms of tradable securities) leads not so much to managed or manageable obligations as to a state of permanent and worsening indebtedness. From this point of view, debt is the very engine of the politics of neoliberalism, a politics which, far from having a simple economic rationale, is for Lazzarato more fundamentally about power: specifically, the radical polarisation of creditors and debtors on a vast scale, such that it is the principle of *asymmetry* rather than the economic idea of exchange or equivalence that dominates neoliberal social and political relations. Today, 'debt is a universal power relation, since everyone is included in it', even – and perhaps especially – those around the world who are too poor to afford credit or receive welfare (p. 32).

The granting of so-called independence to central banks, which in effect guarantees ever deepening recourse to private creditors, means it is now virtually impossible to address public debt through monetary mechanisms. This in turn strengthens the reliance of the state upon the market, to the extent that we have consistently seen governments not only opening themselves up to financial institutions but playing a key role in, as Lazzarato puts it, 'establishing the organizations and structures needed for them to thrive' (p. 26), by ensuring financial deregulation in general and by contributing in particular to developing the range and volume of public-sector securities made attractive to private investors. Against this background, recent austerity measures are in fact double-edged. On the one hand, they seem to be about restricting welfare expenditure in the interests of debt reduction on the part of the state. On the other hand, however, by extending the privatisation of welfare services as an ostensibly cost-cutting exercise, they position welfare provision as part of the very same 'sell-off' which has itself produced the situation that austerity measures are supposed to address and resolve. Thus the austerity politics associated with the sovereign debt crisis are not so much a defiant response to the global debt economy; they are themselves a feature of it.

Equally, to the extent that bail-outs underwritten by the resources of nation states draw upon funds, virtual or otherwise, that circulate or arise in precisely the same financialised structure, based on securitised, tradable debt, they do not signify a reassertion of state power over transnational capital, but on the contrary indicate a further technique to syphon off public money to support a largely privatised system of interests. At such a point, where all money is nothing but debt, monetary sovereignty means very little, and has in any case been greatly eroded over the past few decades by the newly forged neoliberal alliance between the state and private interests and by the policies this demands.[3] Recalling Nietzsche's reminder of the etymological interplay of debts (*Schulden*) and guilt (*Schuld*), Lazzarato argues that the subsequent moralisation of debt allows guilt to be more or less violently attributed to the debtor rather than the creditor, whether it be the unemployed, students, the Greeks or whoever. And this in turn, he insists, allows control not only of the debtor's present, but all of their time to come, establishing an 'economy of time' in which the future is reduced to the expression and experience of 'a society without time, without possibility' (p. 47).

Drawing on the work of Deleuze and Guattari, Lazzarato insists that the debt economy necessitates a theory of money as, first of all, debt-money. According to such a view, money itself arises neither on the strength of the exchange relations required by the circulation of the commodity, nor as an expression of the surplus value extracted from labour. Instead, money is to be understood first of all as a sign of the radical asymmetry of power. (Although I do not want to reprise the problem here, recall that in Graeber there is the suggestion of a similar position being taken at times although, due to other aspects of his approach to the topic, such indications are not entirely unequivocal.) Thus Lazzarato writes:

> Money is first of all debt-money, created *ex nihilo*, which has no material equivalent other than its power to destroy/create social relations and, in particular, modes of subjectivation. (p. 35)

In fact, the latter is seen as a crucial aspect of such power. A key feature of the asymmetrical force of power from which money as debt-money derives is the 'power to prescribe and impose modes of future exploitation, domination, and subjection' (pp. 34–5). Debt-money, in other words, determines, delimits, commands and controls the future as much as the present. And it does so, Lazzarato argues, not just for states or societies in general, but for individuals in their psychic and existential forms, embodied in the subjective presence of 'indebted man'.

As the radical asymmetry of power finds its echo and confirmation in infinite and irredeemable debt – one that simultaneously must and cannot be repaid – 'indebted man', as both a universal and an individual figure, comes to the fore. Once again, Nietzsche is followed in that the relation of religion (specifically Christianity) to the capitalist debt economy is carefully traced. Alluding to Nietzsche, Lazzarato suggests that such a 'man' is the one who first of all must *promise* or must vouch for himself in the future – although he restricts the meaning of such promising (which he acknowledges is the 'promise of future value') to an avowed obligation to repay. In other words, the man who 'is able to *stand guarantor* for himself' is, here, simply the one who is 'capable of honouring his debt' (pp. 39–40). This formulation reduces somewhat the rather more complicated story Nietzsche tells about the rise of the 'sovereign individual' in the complex interstices of reactive slavish morality and active life. Be that as it may, Lazzarato draws upon Nietzschean thought (specifically, the second essay of the *Genealogy of Morals*, which as you'll recall Graeber dismisses as merely a period-bound spoof), principally to aid his argument that 'modern-day capitalism seems to have discovered on its own the technique described by Nietzsche of constructing a person capable of promising' (p. 42) and thus of *owing*. Since, for Lazzarato, such debt should be understood at its source as fundamentally non-economic – that is, based on the irreducible asymmetry of power rather than the transactional equivalences of exchange – such promising entails a liability which no future could ever redeem, but which will if anything only intensify in times to come. Put differently, as Lazzarato writes a little later on (according to an argument which is forcefully repeated on several occasions):

> Finance is a formidable instrument for controlling the temporality of action, neutralizing possibilities, the 'moving present', 'quivering uncertainty' and 'the line where past and future meet.' It locks up possibilities within an established framework while at the same time projecting them into the future. For finance, then, the future is a mere forecast of current domination and exploitation. (p. 71)

I want to suggest that Lazzarato's argument, stridently reasserted as it is, is somewhat complicit with the 'force' or 'power' it seeks to critique, in that it leaves untouched two questions with which Nietzsche's own text struggles (questions that, in his rush to identify the text as merely *of its time*, Graeber sorely neglects in Nietzsche): first, the – theoretical – question of origins, poorly served and rather tellingly neglected at the point that Lazzarato's intimates the more or less accidental discovery by 'modern-day capitalism' of the 'technique' of debt; and, second, relatedly, the question of the conditions of the future, which throughout *The Making of Indebted Man* is constructed merely as the self-identical possibility of mastery projecting itself along an infinite horizon, without difference or remainder. This is a future altogether divested of its temporal flux or uncertainty. For Lazzarato, needless to say, this is the true aim of neoliberalism, but I want to suggest that such a 'truth' is far from incontestable.

These questions are strongly interrelated, of course, not just in the obvious sense that both the past and the future imply temporality in its most general sense, or in the banal sense that causal or teleological thought of all kinds (including some varieties of Marxism) typically assumes one to depend upon the other. More specifically, they are interrelated to the degree that the text on which Lazzarato bases the conceptual elements of his argument – the second essay of the *Genealogy* – is itself shot through with the uncertain question of retroactivity. For Nietzsche, this concerns the error of mixing up and muddling together the 'origin' and the 'aim' of something, when, as he himself puts it:

> there is a world of difference between the reason for something coming into existence in the first place and the ultimate use to which it is put . . . anything which exists, once it has somehow come into being, can be reinterpreted in the service of new intentions, repossessed, repeatedly modified to a new use by a power superior to it . . . all overpowering and mastering is a reinterpretation, a manipulation in the course of which the previous 'meaning' and 'aim' must necessarily be obscured or effaced.[4]

As we will see, it is possible to argue that the question of retroactivity is absolutely inseparable from the problem of debt with which Nietzsche struggles. This leads to certain weaknesses or omissions in Lazzarato's treatment of debt. In particular, it is troubling that Lazzarato's analysis only pays scant critical or philosophical attention to the question of the future and the past, the 'aim' and the 'origin', viewing them largely as extended forms of the present (which may be more or less projected from the 'now'), and that he fails to think them according to the highly complicated and perhaps irresolvable structure of retroactivity which – so Nietzsche's text implies as much as contends – makes possible the very horizon or appearance of debt. If granting credit opens one up to future 'uncertainty', as he puts it, Lazzarato nevertheless insists rather emphatically that the 'system of debt' must 'neutralize time': 'that is the risk inherent to it' (p. 45). Money as capital thus 'pre-empts the future' (p. 74), such that to talk of a present crisis is misleading in that it suggests some hope of resolution or escape, whereas in all likelihood, Lazzarato suggests, we are in the midst of an irreversible and permanent catastrophe (p. 151). But if, as Nietzsche suggests (on occasion, despite himself), debt exists for us or appears to us as part of time's 'uncertainty' – indeed, if it takes the very form of time's uncertainty – one wonders how debt could ever secure and extend itself unproblematically beyond time, simply appropriating or objectivising time according to its own needs. How could debt survive without the remainder of a problem that is arguably intrinsic to its make-up, and which in fact only redoubles throughout debt's perhaps inescapably retroactive interpretation? From this perspective, it appears that the question of the future is actually pre-empted by Lazzarato himself, as much as it is by 'money as capital'. A further question concerns the relation of debt and sovereignty, particularly in regard to the proposition of a calculable future. To be subjected to such a logic of calculability – which, since it reduces the subject's 'contractual' relation to the state, is not simply of the order of the 'economic', being instead, Lazzarato would say, evidence of a power in force – certainly seems to attest to slavish reactivity: the pervasive figure of 'indebted man' who foolishly tries to economise with a debt that really only attests to such a power. But, even if we grant it a non- or aneconomic 'origin', one wonders if such calculation is truly becoming for the master. In Nietzschean terms, does the apprehensive need to control the future genuinely testify to the absolute self-will, the proud aggressivity and warlike venturing of the sovereign? Or does it tie him, instead, to the seemingly unbreakable structure of creditor and debtor? Put another way, on the basis of the intellectual grounds or resources of his own argument, one might ask whether Lazzarato's God-like figure of the ultimate Creditor presiding over universal debt throughout the catastrophic time of a future-without-future is really a tenable one, in terms of its philosophical consistency.[5] There may be a divisible or non-self-identical core to the very structure and temporality of debt, one that could prove useful in thinking about its limits and the possible resistance to it (more so than Lazzarato's rather poorly theorised allusions to capitalism's contradictions or to a Nietzschean 'second innocence').

Nietzschean Debts

In the second essay of Nietzsche's *On the Genealogy of Morals*, the principle of *ressentiment* that characterises the profound break with aristocratic values through the slave revolt in morality is seen to operate on the basis of retroactivity. As such, the values derived through *ressentiment* are retrospectively posited as original. For Nietzsche, of course, slavish nature opts for vengefulness towards noble and higher life as a means of compensation for its own weakness and impotence. Whereas the noble spirit places plenitude and self-reliance at the heart of aristocratic values, slavishness can do no more than found its moral system on the resentful rejection of higher life, in a way that reduces its capacity for action to the purely reactive. The image of the powerful man as the origin of evil justifies the wholly reactive moral schema of slavish life – an origin that, Nietzsche suggests, is constituted retroactively in order to compensate for its own dissolute inadequacy.

For instance, through its account of *ressentiment*, the *Genealogy* questions the historical origins of justice as grounded in a sanctified notion of revenge, as if justice were simply a mechanism for righting wrongs or, in other words, an apt expression of reactive feeling. For Nietzsche, justice develops not from the vengefulness that always supplements a concern for fairness or rights. Instead, it emanates from what is most active in the noble spirit, namely 'the really *active* feelings, such as the desire to dominate, to possess, and the like' (p. 55). Justice, then, originates in nothing more than 'the good will that prevails among those of roughly equal power to come to terms with each other' – that is each other's 'really *active* feelings' – through forms of economic and military settlement bringing war to an end in circumstances of evenly matched force or capacity (in the process, imposing this settlement on all those less powerful). In fact, Nietzsche suggests that 'the active and aggressive forces' compel a settlement in this manner – that is, as an instance of good will among the powerful, rather than an abstractly conceived levelling in the interests of fairness or right – 'in part to contain and moderate the extravagance of reactive pathos', and to stop the spread of its 'senseless raging'. Indeed, it is to oppose the resentful interpretation of justice – justice as that which seeks redress for an injured party (an interpretation derived retroactively on behalf of injured parties) – that law itself is established. However, from this point of view, the justice meted out by law is not a matter of intrinsic right, not a case of 'right and wrong *as such*'; instead, 'legal conditions' put into historic operation 'exceptional states of emergency, partial restrictions which the will to life in its quest for power provisionally imposes on itself in order to serve its overall goal: the creation of *larger* units of power' fundamentally unchecked by reactive feeling (pp. 56–7).

If in its emphasis on the constitutive character of power this line of argument chimes well with Lazzarato's own, it is nevertheless important to recognise at its centre a clear connection between reactive morality (debt) and retroactivity. Reactive life is served by the retroactive explanation of origins, in a way that is not dissimilar to the retroactivity of the traumatic origin with which Freud struggles in 'The Wolf-Man' (the idea that the origin may be generated retrospectively by the neurotic's phantasmatic desire). Perhaps most importantly, retroactivity is not just one means among others to develop the interests of slavish life. Instead, through its own complicated structure of guilt-debt, it is perhaps the very form reactive feeling takes. As Nietzsche writes, the attempt to 'sanctify *revenge* under the name of justice . . . as if justice were merely an extension of the feeling of injury' posits revenge as the basis for bringing 'all the *reactive* feelings retroactively to a position of honour' (p. 54). To the extent that its devotion to revenge is unremitting, unrelenting, pitiless, the retroactive honouring of reactive feelings not only upholds and expresses the morality of the slave (bondage to debt or vengeful reactive/economistic thought); more fundamentally, it seems indissociable from the character of reactive feeling itself.

By its very title, of course, the essay in which these observations occur concerns itself with 'guilt', 'bad conscience' and 'related matters'. Nietzsche begins the essay by noting that active forgetfulness is a particular strength of the man of noble spirit. It contributes to his '*robust health*' – notably in contrast to those who, like dyspeptics, are 'never through with anything'. Nonetheless, a 'counter-faculty' now adds itself to this 'strength': a form of memory that wills the suspension of active forgetting. This form of memory is allied to the 'promising' that, from the outset of the text, seems to draw 'man' into his own definition. Someone who makes a promise, Nietzsche tells us, does so in order 'that finally he would be able to vouch for himself *as future*' (p. 40). In the sense that the promiser assigns his name to a promise to open a line of credit to the future, in his own mind 'man' has made himself '*calculable, regular, necessary*'. The '*memory of the will*' is, it seems, as much a feature of this calculability as the effort to 'dispose of the future in advance' that, in a certain way, promising seeks to affirm. This aspect of Nietzsche's essay is, of course, heavily emphasised in Lazzarato's argument.

Indeed, Nietzsche opens the second section of the essay by describing the interaction he has just suggested between memory and promise in terms of 'the long history of *responsibility*' (p. 40). Here, he adds that the calculability of 'man' as the subject of this very same responsibility depends not just upon the uniformity or consistency of the past, present and future in the 'life' of an individual, but also upon a regularity or uniformity *among* men, so that each is 'an equal among equals'. If this implies the very seeds of slavish morality and reactive feeling ('the morality of custom and the social strait-jacket'), nevertheless 'by way of contrast' Nietzsche points us towards 'the other end of this enormous process' – the very possibility of the '*sovereign individual*' no longer constrained by custom. Through 'special consciousness of power and freedom', such a man grasps more genuinely his own self-sufficiency. He can truly vouch for himself, and on this basis is entitled to promise. Thus, as previously suggested, the 'man' who *promises* emerges in the more complex interstices of active and slavish life. However, the type of equality demanded by reactive feeling is in one sense eschewed, to the extent that this sovereign individual 'respects those who are like him' only insofar as they, too, are capable of imposing their superiority upon lesser, more contemptible beings – in particular those 'dogs' and 'liars' who abuse their promises. Here, as Lazzarato affirms (following Deleuze and Guattari), sheer power precedes economic measure.

Nietzsche traces within this history of responsibility the origin of con- science. The point at which this word occurs – the transition from the second to the third section of the essay – also sees a return to the theme of wilful memory as indispensable to the self-affirmation Nietzsche wishes to celebrate. If it is possible to think that, in order to forge memo- ries for himself, man learnt that 'the most powerful aid to memory was pain', nonetheless Nietzsche also laments the long-enduring nature of that 'psychology' which, conceiving of remembrances as 'branded' upon the mind, equates recollection with the persistence of a certain hurt (p. 43). If the origins of asceticism are to be found in this doctrine of painful memory, it is also, Nietzsche implies, the founding myth of, for instance, Germanicism itself. As such, it is backed by a litany of cruel punishments designed for those who, among or indeed *by dint of* their various crimes, forget their Germanness. By the fourth section of the essay, however, Nietzsche finds firmer footing in the question of 'bad conscience' or guilt. Here, 'our genealogists of morals' are of no use, in large part because they think retroactively, imputing origins in terms of derived values and thus showing themselves incapable of comprehending a past that does not reflect their own moral schemas. As such, they lack the 'second sight', as Nietzsche puts it, which would allow them to trace the moral idea of guilt (*Schuld*) back to its more material origins in the concept of debt (*schulden*). Consequently, Nietzsche insists that punishment as a form of repayment developed prior to, and thus outside of, the attribution of blame, which only imposed itself much later in human history. Before this, he argues, punishment was not meted out soberly to repay guilt, but occurred as an apt expression of anger – one that, rather than overflowing itself in wholly gratuitous cruelty, running to the very limit of its power, was 'held in check and modified' by an equivalence between transgressive damage and the retributive pain which the punisher imputed to the punishment itself.

Punishment, then, took its meaning and definition – its specific form *as* punishment rather than mere violence – not from guilt, but from anger. And yet the very need to constitute punishment *as* punishment, leading as it did to the 'idea of an equivalence between damage and pain', gives force to the contractual form punishment takes as an expression of the sort of exchange relationship one finds between creditor and debtor. Lazzarato, of course, disputes precisely this contractual or exchange form of debt, pointing instead to the more original context of those power relations which, as Nietzsche himself suggests, make 'anger' possible. Yet, at this point in Nietzsche's argument, one may well ask whether contract or exchange establishes itself as the necessary context for a sense of injury or – vice versa – whether the experience of harm provides the explanation for the emergence of economic or contractual forms and practices of all kinds. Is it that 'to repay' is first of all to repay harm done, as Nietzsche himself suggests, so that forms of exchange arise from the prior or more original experience of pain (as perhaps foremost a consequence of power)? Or, alternatively, is the very experience of pain, harm or damage ever possible outside of the very concept of injury that, Nietzsche tells us, stokes reactive feeling? (The latter, of course, is funded by a strongly economistic sense of fairness and equality.) If debts to the past are remembered only upon risk or threat of pain, or if the pledge to repay is from ancient times underwritten by the possibility of harsh bodily sacrifice, is it that pain makes possible the sense of debt and indebtedness? (Is debt indebted to pain?) Or, conversely, does the very possibility of pain emerge only on the strength of a certain set of economic relations? To the extent that this conundrum persists so as to raise once more the problem of retroactive thinking, is it the case that Nietzschean thought leaves this matter unresolved as a way to free itself from the retroactive impulse – and thus to rejoice in a time before slavish reactivity, which may in fact only serve Nietzsche's own 'retroactive' needs? Or is it that Nietzsche falters before and thus remains embroiled in the snares of reactive-retroactive thinking? On this basis, one might speculate about whether the *Genealogy* remains painfully caught in, and thus cruelly indebted to, just that form of thought it seeks to critique or surpass, and hence whether it proves impossible to approach the question of debt outside of retroactivity's traps.

In the fifth section of his essay, Nietzsche draws attention to the loosening of a strict equivalence between unrestituted debt and the commensurate bodily sacrifice as, for him, the welcome consequence of a '*more Roman* conception of law' (p. 46).[6] Thus the 'logic of this whole form of exchange' undergoes a certain shift, whereby instead of the extent of the repayable sum being construed by way of the stringent measure of actual flesh, recompense is to be calculated in terms of the extraction of pleasure in the other's suffering. True, the extent of the gratification may have been thought to intensify depending on the relative social rankings of debtor and creditor (the more lowly the creditor and more highly ranked the debtor, the greater the delight in inflicting 'punishment'), so that the precise value of the pleasure in another's distress was calibrated, variably, according to class position. Nevertheless, it would seem that this at least partial departure from what looked to be a more strictly reactive system of compensation, in as much as it entailed what Nietzsche terms 'the entitlement and right to cruelty', introduced the distinct possibility of a (perhaps more original) uneconomic or aneconomic element into the economy of credit and debt. For surely cruelty distinguishes itself from revenge in that it irreducibly includes a gratuitous supplement – even if in the Spinozist formulation of 'disinterested malice' – that would seem to better serve the sovereign aggressivity of noble life, rather than purely reactive slavish morals? As Nietzsche observes, by means of a 'punishment' based on pleasure extracted from pain rather than on a measure of flesh commensurate with the size of the debt, 'the creditor partakes of a *privilege of the masters*', so that regardless of the specific identity of creditor or debtor, the system serves the noble spirit rather than slavish life (pp. 46–7).

Here, then, the main tenor of Lazzarato's arguments, based on the idea of the foremost concerns of power, seems to echo Nietzsche's own directions of thought. For if 'man' is indeed *the* 'measuring animal', if he is developed within and by means of systems of exchange, value and price, nevertheless this is not the whole story, or at any rate the story is far from a simple one. For while such apparent economism determines the very possibility of man's self-estimation and astuteness – his 'thinking as such', Nietzsche ventures to say – nevertheless the principle of mastery which in one sense impels such economistic thinking and practice implies nevertheless the extraction of a surplus that cannot simply be reassimilated to the narrow world of economic values (though, for all that, it is a crucial part of it): 'man's feeling of superiority' (p. 51). This is because – as the example of a law that is *'more Roman'* implies – the sense of masterful privilege or sovereign aggressivity extracts its supplement of 'superiority' precisely by resisting the more purely economistic attitude of reactive feeling. Somewhat paradoxically, then, this 'noble' surplus is able to assert its value in and over a social world defined by economic exchange, by dint of the very fact that it cannot be wholly determined by it. It is perhaps the fact that one cannot easily economise with this paradox that reinforces the enigmatic power of the master.

Yet such an aneconomic remainder of economy finds its mirror image in the power, not simply to forgive rather than punish transgressions, but to overlook them altogether. Such power is perhaps closely allied to the ability to decide exemptions or exceptions to the law, the very same law which, as we've already seen, is in any case nothing but an 'exceptional state' designed to partially restrict sovereign will only to furnish its ultimate ambitions more effectively, not least by mediating and thus lessening the 'reactive' resentments of injured parties. Despite the seemingly inexorable pattern of credit and debt which determines social relations *tout court*, therefore, Nietzsche observes that the developed power of the community attests to itself insofar as it no longer needs to punish its debtors – those who, according to a variety of misdeeds, transgress against the community by breaking or by failing to acknowledge their contractual obligation to it. Put differently, sovereign power is in fact the power to *eschew* debt, to decide against the (reactive) logic of 'everything must be paid off'.

This feature of Nietzsche's argument is not sufficiently acknowledged by Lazzarato, even though it fits with his insistence on the non-economic origin of debt. To overlook debt – to ignore the transgressor's 'default', their un-repaid indebtedness – is to demonstrate that one is powerful enough to survive the 'loss' without need of recompense in the (economic) form of a substitution: punishment for debt. It is to assert that one is powerful enough to transcend the exchange-form of life. Indeed, on this basis great strength is affirmed, not threatened, by an ever increasing amount of unpaid debt. Once again, the 'noble' supplement extracted by the master in this state of affairs is in one sense a part or feature of and yet irreducible to the 'economy' that is a principal instrument of power (albeit a power that is asymmetric and thus aneconomic in originary terms). Once more, one might contend, this very same paradox lies at the heart of the enigma of sovereignty. Yet such a paradox keeps open the question of whether recourse to the debt economy – immersion in debtor–creditor relations, whether partial or not – simply enhances or also jeopardises the creditor as a figure of mastery or sovereignty. Perhaps it does both at the same time.

The folly of retroactive thinking is made most explicit in section twelve of the essay, where Nietzsche warns against the error of confusing or conflating the 'origin' with the 'aim' of punishment. As we saw above, he writes:

> there is a world of difference between the reason for something coming into existence in the first place and the ultimate use to which it is put . . . anything which exists, once it has somehow come into being, can be reinterpreted in the service of new intentions, repossessed, repeatedly modified to a new use by a power superior to it . . . all overpowering and mastering is a reinterpretation, a manipulation in the course of which the previous 'meaning' and 'aim' must necessarily be obscured or effaced. (p. 58)

Since, from the perspective of the will to power, history is not the story of causal development or progression, but instead one of a succession of more or less violent overturnings, the most rigorous and astute analysis of the usage of a thing, or of its 'aims' in the present, is poorly served by the tendency to impute an 'origin' based upon the (extended) terms of this same analysis – although, of course, the distortion this implies is never just a weakness, in the sense that such misrepresentation is also part of the project of 'overpowering' and 'mastering' that such 'reinterpretation' itself serves. If this looks to be a case of taking from one hand to give to another (i.e. strengthening and weakening oneself in equal measure), nevertheless it is not quite the same as robbing Peter to pay Paul, because what is involved is not a zero-sum game. Instead, there is a definite *interest* at stake. If the reactive morality of the slave implies a near interminable debt, retroactive thinking extracts a surplus in precisely this form of interest, making the debt work to its credit. Indeed, the use of the word 'repossessed', at any rate in the English translation, is interesting here. The German is somewhat more colloquial and violent. *Neu in Beschlag genommen* suggests being taken over anew, although *Beschlag* is constructed from the verb to strike (*schlagen*). The overall meaning is not so much that of 'repossession' in the English sense, which suggests the legally settled restitution of goods or property to the original owner, but rather forever being violently overpowered, mastered, 'struck', albeit struck or forced into service rather than being physically accosted more directly. Still, to the extent that it implies at once an inability to repay debts and a refusal to overlook or write them off, 'repossession' strikes our interest, notably through its kinship with retroactivity. Retroactive reappropriation of the meaning of an 'origin' at once acknowledges and denies it. It denies the 'origin', by more or less violently transforming its meaning 'in the service of new intentions', but it nevertheless acknowledges it, if only in the form of the reactive feeling which repeatedly encounters or confronts the 'origin' as an almost interminable source of injury, and thus a constant source of debit or debt. Indeed, to deny (indebtedness to) the 'origin' in the form of reinterpreting it, while reinterpreting it as the basis for a pervasive sense of liability, debit or debt – a debt from which, nevertheless, perhaps untold *credit* or *interest* may be extracted – all this suggests the highly complex debt economy of retroactive thinking/reactive life.

The Nietzschean economy of debt is further complicated and reinforced by what we might term its diachronic axis, whereby the indebtedness of the present generation to its forefathers increases as the community prospers, having more and more to be thankful for. For Nietzsche, as the community advances, its debts become almost irredeemable. Once more, the debt-form of social life reaches a certain zenith only at the point of near insolvency: that stage at which, in order to be settled, debts could perhaps only ever be written off. While Nietzsche suggests that those of truly noble quality repay their forefathers with *interest* (the obvious paradox here hardly needs remarking) (p. 70), nevertheless it is difficult in this context not to think the contrary (à la Lazzarato): namely that the effort to repay *even and perhaps especially if it is massive* only deepens the debt. Nietzsche writes of periodic 'large lump' repayments (cruel sacrifices and the like) which, since they not only foreground the extent of the debt but also powerfully underline 'the *fear* of the forefather and his power' (until he is, famously, 'transfigured into a *god*'), serve not to lessen or ameliorate but to inflate the debt further, raising the stakes of the entire situation. Yet this spiralling debt does not paralyse the community; on the contrary, it is just a sign of its prosperity and strength, becoming 'ever-more victorious, independent, respected, feared' (p. 69).

For sure, the desire to redeem what is owed, and sometimes even to mimic the gods, persists so as to complicate the credit-debt structure of the community. In addition, as Nietzsche speculates, perhaps rather naively, the dramatic rise of atheism may come to liberate mankind from a sense of indebtedness. Nevertheless, that 'the sense of guilt towards the divinity has continued to grow for several thousands of years' testifies to the long-standing and near intractable debt structure of modern society. In fact, within the space of a few lines, Nietzsche seems to backtrack on his dream of a '*second innocence*' born of aesthetic feeling, lamenting that 'the real situation is fearfully different'. Indeed, despite the millennial tone of the essay's last section, which dreams of the redeeming-godless 'man of the future', Nietzsche is still to be found saying that, in the current circumstances, 'an attempt at reversal would *in itself* be impossible'. In a line that is all the more striking for its contemporary resonance, he asserts: 'The *goal* now is the pessimistic one of closing off once and for all the prospect of a definitive repayment.' An 'iron possibility' takes hold through the ever more intransigent imposition of an undischargeable duty, a remorseless guilt, 'eating its way in, spreading down and out like a polyp'. No penance would be enough to atone, no repayment enough to compensate (pp. 71–5).

All of this would seem to be grist to Lazzarato's mill. However, in an ironic final twist of expropriation, even the creditor – the master, the god – is at last swept into this nightmarish scenario of total debt. As Nietzsche enigmatically hints, the forefather becomes Adam, divine banishment incarnate. This does not result in the prospect of revolutionary change but instead ushers in a godless afterlife, 'essentially devoid of value', in which the story of the gods' fall from grace is – as pure expediency – retold in terms of Christ's sacrifice: God becomes man, takes man's place, so that if he succumbs to (indebted) man's plight at all, it is only to redeem his guilt, all guilt (p. 72). By such means, however, God himself seeks redress, seeks to redeem or re-place himself, to restore his credit. In other words, as Nietzsche puts it, he is to be found 'paying himself off'. Perhaps only a God can so blithely write off debt, even his own, but still one wonders whether this leaves him purely 'in the black'. Through the enigma of God's self-torture on the cross (a self-torture which, perhaps by way of ironic reversal, seems to mimic the torments of slavish life), does such a death cancel all debts to the absolute credit of the divine? Or does it signal, too, just this fall into a whole world of debt, indeed a world that is so debt-ridden it is by now almost *beyond* debt, one which survives therefore only as 'nihilistic renunciation', 'essentially devoid of value'? Nietzsche does not exactly tell the story this way, as this part of the essay develops, preferring instead to concentrate on man's slavish torments before a God to whom all is owed (cruelly felt as 'real', 'incarnate'). But lingering, ghost-like in his text is the possibility that just this debt – in all its impossible cruelty – is premised in the end upon the *spectrality* of an ultimate Creditor. In view of this phantasmatic scene, the debate into which Nietzsche enters in the last section of the essay – whether or not his writing sets up anew or forever breaks into pieces 'the shrine' of an ideal – seems a little beside the point. For Nietzsche's text suggests that to bring down or to set up a new God may be part of the same picture. One wonders what such an insight would do to the dream or vision of a 'conqueror of God and of nothingness' yet to come, with which the text concludes.

On the basis of this reading of Nietzsche two objections arise to Lazzarato's thesis. First, his idea of a catastrophic future-without-future of permanent debt depends on the analysis of an ever intensifying asymmetry of power that elevates the creditor to near-Godlike status. While this suggestion clearly derives from a certain strand of thought in Nietzsche's *Genealogy*, the perhaps more radical implication of a debt so pervasive that it leaves no creditor intact suggests ways to think about the non-self-identical or divisible limits of sovereignty and sovereign debt. Second, and relatedly (since it implies a question of the future, which Lazzarato tells us sovereign debt has cancelled entirely), the idea that the retroactivity so central to the possibility of debt itself is based on a false continuity between past and present, 'origin' and 'aim', suggests in turn that debt itself (in the form of reactivity-retroactivity) aggresses against temporal continuity in general. If this is true, then debt's supposed commitment to the unstinting continuity and continuation of the present for all future time to come (as an unbreakable expression of power) itself becomes questionable and resistible, not just as an idea but in terms of the practical possibilities suggested by the limit or deficit between what it *wants* and what it *is*: in other words, its retroactivity. Once more, such a possibility arises despite some of the more dominant flourishes of Nietzsche's remarks. Taken together, these objections to the oversimplified conceptions of sovereignty and temporality in Lazzarato's book point towards other possibilities, other scenarios in neoliberalism's future, than the ones he is prepared to admit. Thinking, then, both of Graeber and Lazzarato, we might arrive at the following conclusion. Where the question of debt is concerned, taking retroactivity seriously, taking it on board rather than simply dismissing or rejecting it, may prove surprisingly productive for the times to come.

Notes

1. David Graeber, *Debt: The First 5,000 Years* (New York: Melville House, 2011). Further page references appear within the main body of the chapter.
2. Maurizio Lazzarato, *The Making of Indebted Man: An Essay on the Neoliberal Condition*, trans. Joshua David Jordan (Amsterdam: Semiotext(e), 2012). Further page references appear within the main body of the chapter.
3. In his third chapter, 'The Ascendancy of Debt in Neoliberalism', Lazzarato also suggests ways in which sovereignty has been transformed by debt in terms of its disciplinary and biopolitical horizons and practices.
4. Friedrich Nietzsche, *On the Genealogy of Morals*, trans. Douglas Smith (Oxford: Oxford University Press, 2008), p. 58. Further page references

appear within the main body of the chapter.

5. Much could be said of Lazzarato's own debts, not just to Nietzsche, the legacy of the Frankfurt School and other varieties of twentieth-century theory, but also to autonomism and the demands of a post-autonomist account of capital.

6. In sections six and seven of the *Genealogy*, Nietzsche suggests that the bloodiest festivities of cruelty and torture – to the extent that they rehearse not just the possibility of the advent of 'man' but also the theodical interpretation of suffering, which in turn makes possible the 'invention of "free will"' (if only to alleviate the boredom of the gods when confronted with a too-deterministic world) – establish a context for the emergence of 'conscience' and 'guilt'. They do so partly in the sense that cruelty – albeit despite itself – eventually bred shame and, under the increasing 'spell of society and peace' (p. 64), a sickly sensitivity to pain, which for Nietzsche was readily harnessed to the benefit of reactive moral schemas (pp. 49–51). Here, man is afflicted by an inner consciousness, or a 'soul', repelled by the freedom and wildness of the truly active life, and he turns against himself, he suffers from himself and is cruel to himself. This is the form 'bad conscience' takes: its morality is not unselfish or 'unegoistic' but based, somewhat differently, on a 'will to mistreat oneself' (p. 68). However, at the same time Nietzsche is suspicious of attempts to explain the origin or emergence of guilt in terms of practices of punishment, arguing that 'broadly speaking, punishment hardens and deadens', while 'genuine pangs of conscience are especially rare among criminals and prisoners'. This is partly because, for Nietzsche, punishment – at least in its pre-historical phase – displays no interest in reinforcing blame but merely seeks to respond to the fact of harm, which may have occurred regardless of the intentions of the culprit. Such punishment in fact serves to detach the criminal from a sense of responsibility for his actions, promotes fatalism, and so actually hinders the sense of guilt (p. 62). Meanwhile, in section seventeen, Nietzsche asserts that 'bad conscience' can be traced back to the violent reduction and suppression of freedom caused by the active force of sovereign individuals: in other words, the will to power.

Chapter 5

Survival of Cruelty

*René Girard reported to me that after my lecture in Baltimore
. . . Lacan supposedly replied: 'Yes, yes, it's good, but the
difference between him and me is that he does not deal with
people who are suffering', meaning by that: people in analysis.
What did he know about that? Very careless. To be able to say
such a thing, so imperturbably, and know such a thing, he
could not have been referring either to suffering (alas, I too
deal with people who suffer – all of you, for example) or to
transference, that is, to love, which has never needed the
analytic situation to claim its victims.*

(Jacques Derrida, 'For the Love of Lacan')[1]

What, after all, is cruelty? How may it be interpreted or analysed, and
by whom? How is it to be determined or delimited, and to whose understanding does it 'properly' belong? How would this relationship, this
'affair', manifest itself? What is the relation, for instance, not only of
psychoanalysis *to* cruelty, but of psychoanalysis *and* cruelty? The latter
– psychoanalysis *and* cruelty – would perhaps imply not only the question of the relations of domination between them, but a larger discourse,
lexicon or economy (if it is indeed an 'economy' at all, if economy *and*
cruelty could ever attain such identity) which may comprise them, or
indeed overhang and thus constitutively exceed them, or for that matter
succumb to, fall foul of them in some manner. Dominating *or* dominated by them (psychoanalysis *and* cruelty), the very idea of such an
(S-M?) 'economy' – lexical, discursive or otherwise – therefore already
suggests the possibility of a certain cruelty, one whose conceptual
borders remain, however, sufficiently indistinct that it can perhaps no
more dominate than be dominated.

What, after all, is cruelty? On several occasions in 'Psychoanalysis
Searches the States of Its Soul: The Impossible Beyond of a Sovereign

Cruelty'[2] Derrida confesses or professes (confesses or professes, since the question of the 'truth' of cruelty is, precisely, at issue here, as well as that of the *cruel* forms both profession and confession might take, in truth) – Derrida confesses or professes his deep uncertainty about the meaning of the term. Cruelty, like sovereignty, resists (we'll have cause to return to this): '*Cruelty, sovereignty, resistance*: I am not at all sure that I know, or even that it is known in general, what these words mean', or, more pertinently perhaps, what they are 'made to mean', for instance in common use or in their psychoanalytic usage (p. 242). *Made* to mean: the irreducible cruelty, perhaps, of meaning itself (wherein the 'resistance' by which the term 'cruelty' resists 'meaning' itself participates in this same problem, a problem of cruelty perhaps). It is only ever 'as if we knew the meaning of this word' (p. 238), as if, indeed, our own understanding or the agreement among ourselves about what cruelty actually *meant* might be sufficiently permeated by cruelty itself as to become unreliable, hence somehow less than cruel – or, rather, more cruel than cruel perhaps. When Derrida says, therefore, 'I will spare us any example of this cruelty' (p. 240) – a cruelty, however, which in our own time might be 'the most unprecedented and most inventive' (even if we are in the midst of a 'growing struggle against the vestiges of forms of punishment called "cruel"' (pp. 244–5), a cruelty about which no 'discourse' other than psychoanalysis stands more ready 'to take an interest', although perhaps at the price of becoming itself 'more indecipherable than ever' (p. 240)) – one wonders whether such unexampled cruelty is spared us due to Derrida's uncertainty about what might indeed constitute cruelty's exemplarity, or whether it is exemplary cruelty that is in fact at stake at the point Derrida 'spares' us – whether cruelly or non-cruelly – from the benefit or 'interest' of the example. The concepts of sovereignty, of cruelty, of resistance, we are told, await 'revolution', revolutionary transformation – whether bloodless or not, cruel or not, it is hard to say, for there is never just one revolution, 'there is always more than one revolution possible in the revolution' (p. 246), meaning perhaps that the meaning of cruelty may – cruelly or not – be no less equivocal after the revolution, whether bloody or bloodless, cruel or non-cruel (the opposition begins to falter, cruelly enough perhaps, as does that between fundamentally bloody and essentially non-bloody cruelty, between the Latin *cruos* and the Germanic – and Freudian – *grausamkeit*).[3] The memory of cruelty is, simply, absolutely 'enormous, bottomless', as Derrida puts it, an archive-without-end that includes Revolutionary Terror, 'the cruelty of the death penalty on a massive scale, the cruelty of all the tortures and executions in the aftermath of the 1917 revolution, the still open list of the most relentless cruelties,

Shoah, genocides, mass deportations', abuses of 'human rights', 'crimes against humanity' . . . (p. 266) – who could name such cruelty, or decide its meaning, without blood on their hands, without culpability (blood-less or not), without adding to the already endless list? Cruelty endlessly mutates – it is perhaps mutation, or the possibility of mutation, itself: 'What remains to be thought *more psychoanalytico* would thus be a mutation of cruelty itself – or at least new historical figures of an ageless cruelty, as old and no doubt older than man' (p. 270).[4] A mutant cruelty that is as inhuman and unhuman, perhaps, as it is all-too-human – something deep in the system that produces (itself as) a species-problem. Where does cruelty begin or end, asks Derrida more than once – this cruelty without apparent beginning or end, defined (and un-defined) by just this 'without'?

And so, asks Derrida once more: 'What does "cruel" mean? Do we have, did Freud have a rigorous concept of the cruelty that, like Nietzsche, he spoke of so much (as regards the death drive, the aggression drive, or sadism, etc.)?' (pp. 262–3). Judging by the extent of the usage of the term cruelty throughout the works of Freud, at any rate in the English translation offered by the Standard Edition, the answer would not be assuredly positive. One would be hard pushed to say that there is a fully worked out theory in Freud that goes overtly by the name or under the heading of cruelty, although cruelty often turns up at moments of 'high theoretical significance', as Freud, in *Three Essays on the Theory of Sexuality*, himself puts it.[5] In fact, Freud uses the explicit terminology of cruelty perhaps less frequently than Derrida implies, and if indeed he understands the 'death drive, the aggression drive, or sadism, etc.' in terms of what is 'cruel', he surely does so only through a certain implicitness, often something of a diversion, or in other words by dint of an '*indirect* stratagem' that in fact constitutes cruelty's relations (the phrase is Derrida's, from 'Psychoanalysis Searches the States of Its Soul' (p. 272)) – an '*indirect* stratagem' to which, after a detour or two, we will have cause to return. Thus, Derrida observes, René Major comments on Freud's use of the word cruelty as occurring only 'under conditions whose essential and organizing ambiguity, I believe, should be stressed' (p. 267). As if ambiguity itself enters into the very definition, or at any rate the very conditions of possibility, of cruelty. (Although belief – 'I believe' – may also be far from exempt from these conditions.)

For instance, on more than one occasion Freud links cruelty to revenge,[6] although the precise relation of the two would presumably rest on the question of the degree to which each are gratuitous. How far can revenge, in contrast to cruelty, be purely a matter of retribution, and thus of calculation? Must it not always include an element of pleasure taken in the pain of the other, a cruel supplement? Similarly, is cruelty always absolutely gratuitous, gratuitous without remainder? Freud tells us that 'cruelty in general comes easily to the childish nature, since the obstacle that brings the instinct for mastery to a halt at another person's pain – namely a capacity for pity – is developed relatively late' (pp. 192–3). If 'pure' cruelty would seem to reside in a gratuitousness characterised by childish lack of pity, nonetheless the fact that cruel impulses arise from 'the instinct for mastery' implies that cruelty – even infant cruelty – is always motivated, that it always takes an interest or a share, always expects a certain repayment or return, and as such that it is never purely gratuitous. (The *OED*, for instance, defines 'gratuitous' as that which is 'done or given for nothing'.) As such, and in general, cruelty and revenge therefore couple together only as non-self-identical doubles, albeit suggesting a doubleness that perhaps always announces the enigmatic presence or quality of cruelty itself.

In his writing on the sexual aberrations and infantile sexuality in *Three Essays on the Theory of Sexuality*, meanwhile, Freud associates cruelty with a sadism that would 'correspond to an aggressive component of the sexual instinct', one which, for him, manifests itself in the 'need' to conquer the object of one's sexual interest or desire 'by means other than the process of wooing', i.e. by violent and forcible means. Masochism – for Freud an 'extension' or 'transformation' of sadism, an example of sadistic aggressivity unable to find its outlet in 'actual life' and thus turned back upon the 'self' – relates of course to the pleasure taken by the sufferer in the pain of such 'maltreatment' and 'humiliation' (p. 158). (Everyone knows the old joke: the masochist says 'hurt me', the sadist says 'no!' – a joke that Deleuze calls stupid since he disputes the idea, derived from a certain Freud, that sadism and masochism constitute an interchangeable or reversible pair, two sides of the same coin, forming instead, from Deleuze's point of view, entirely different 'situations' in which, for example, the appearance of sadistic behaviour in scenes of masochism amounts less to sadism proper than to a function or expression of masochistic needs, drives, relations and practices which, he argues, formulate themselves quite differently than is the case in the economy of sadism.)[7] Freud, however, comments that sadism and masochism 'occupy a special position' among what he calls 'the perversions', 'since the contrast between activity and passivity which lies behind them is among the universal characteristics of sexual life' (p. 159) (a while later he numbers among the complex pairings prompted by sadistic or cruel instincts scopophila and exhibitionism, which 'appear in a sense independently of the erotogenic zones' (p. 192), even if their origin is ultimately as 'erotogenic' as the touch of the skin (pp. 166–9).)

Thus, asserts Freud, the very 'history of human civilization shows beyond any doubt that there is an intimate connection between cruelty and the sexual instinct' (p. 159). To the extent that, for Freud, *everything* may be about the 'sexual instinct', cruelty turns out to be potentially omnipresent, all-pervasive, possibly in operation everywhere and at all times (even, and 'habitually', in the 'same individual': 'a sadist is always at the same time a masochist' (p. 159) asserts Freud, here contra Deleuze, as if – again – cruelty in fact depends on its essential doubleness, contrariness or duplicity, the obvious corollary being that, where such doubleness is found, cruelty is never far behind).[8] Yet 'nothing has been done towards explaining the connection' between cruelty and the sexual instinct, says Freud, 'apart from laying emphasis on the aggressive factor in the libido' which, for some authorities, is just a 'relic of cannibalistic desires' (that is of a particular configuration which combined the libido's aggressivity with a certain 'apparatus' or technique for 'obtaining mastery' (p. 159)). However, the 'perversion' of taking pleasure in pain still receives no satisfactory explanation, insists Freud. Thus cruelty would perhaps form the basis of a theory of everything, but is itself little understood, if at all, and presumably, therefore, it must be at least partially withheld until such time as a more rigorous description permits its inclusion in the psychoanalytic lexicon 'proper'. (Given cruelty's innate duplicity, one doubts whether this was ever going to be possible without overwhelming irony.) The 'impulses to perversion' which 'occur regularly as pairs of opposites' – changing places with one another as much as opposing one other – have a 'high theoretical significance', says Freud, one which will become apparent, however, only 'in conjunction with material which will be brought forward later' (p. 160). Once more, cruelty remains in operation only by means of a delay, diversion or detour to which it must succumb, imposing itself never quite in its own name. From a certain Freudian perspective, perhaps, this might be the masochism of cruelty's sadism – or vice versa – found constantly at work.

The problem of cruelty's meaning or definition, its determination or delimitation, has to do with the fact that, as both Nietzsche and Freud insisted (and indeed foresaw), cruelty seems to be without limit. However, close to the beginning of his essay Derrida suggests that – in contrast to Nietzsche – Freud thought cruelty to be perhaps limitless but 'not without opposable term, that is, endless but not without contrary'. 'This will be one of our questions', states Derrida (p. 239). For sure. But it is a question that remains hidden or implicit throughout the subsequent thirty or so pages (an '*indirect* stratagem'?). For lengthy periods of the remaining text, what cruelty may come to mean no doubt relies on those terms with which cruelty may share some affinity or relationship, but it is a very long time before we are able to glimpse the possibility of this opposable term in its specific form (by which time, I will suggest, the question of what is 'opposable' might have mutated somewhat – cruelly, perhaps, but not only cruelly). Cruelty is, for instance, repeatedly aligned with sovereignty, perhaps in the sense that both are necessarily excessive, exceptional, gratuitous and, thus, beyond a simple logic or law of relation, exchange or calculation that they also instigate or at any rate encourage. Relatedly, the link between cruelty and 'the drive for power' is raised (p. 241), although Derrida tells us this is not his principle question. The question is also raised of the relationship to what is 'cruel' of '*both* the pleasure and reality principles *and* the death or sovereign mastery drives, which seem to be at work wherever cruelty is on the horizon' (p. 241), although Derrida's main interest is in an 'impossible beyond' of this cruelty, which would also take us (impossibly, undecidably) beyond all the figures and forms of Freudian discourse. And yet, as Derrida himself suggests, cruelty itself would seem to be unthinkable without some supplementing form of psychic cruelty, as a cruelty which not only helps define the 'object' of (psycho-)analysis but perhaps also pervades or infects its very *thought*, the very thought of such an 'object'. What is most 'proper' to such psychic cruelty – as 'non-bloody' cruelty, cruelty linked not so much to the Latin root *cruor*, meaning bloody wound, as the Germanic and Freudian *grausamkeit*, entailing suffering which does not essentially depend on the spilling of blood – would no doubt be a matter for psychoanalysis, suggests Derrida. (Although presumably this apparent distinction would surely only reopen, for psychoanalysis, the question of castration's original violence.) Such a 'psychoanalysis' – as the analysis of psychic cruelty – might not necessarily entail an already-given, preconstituted psychoanalysis. It would imply a psychoanalysis transformed from top to bottom by the cruelty that forms its 'proper' object – a 'proper' object, however, that will present itself, perhaps, as a sign of the irreducible possibility of cruelty as much as of (psycho-)analytic self-consolidation or progress.[9] Thus there would be no simple psychoanalysis of cruelty, no psychoanalysis *of* cruelty that didn't register somehow the double genitive which makes cruelty as much the form psychoanalysis takes as the 'object' after which it enquires. Cruelty as indispensable to psychoanalysis in at least a double sense, then, a 'sense' (sense-of-itself) with which psychoanalysis will have to reckon according to a logic or economy that – although possibly cruel through and through – nevertheless remains necessarily obscure.

Derrida, indeed, ventures a 'hypothesis on a hypothesis' (that of the 'proper', although of course always improper, relation of psychoanalysis to cruelty), as follows:

> If there is something irreducible in the life of the living being, in the soul, in the psyche (for I do not limit my remarks to that of the living being called man, and thus I leave suspended the immense and formidable question, an open question in my view, of animality in general, and of whether psychoanalysis is or is not, through and through, an anthropology), and if this irreducible thing in the life of the animate being is indeed the possibility of cruelty . . . then no other discourse . . . could open itself up to this hypothesis. (p. 240)

I omit crucial sections from this sentence (concerning how one might interpret 'the possibility of cruelty' and to which discourses or disciplines we might refer, notably to assure ourselves of the unique resources of psychoanalysis) only in order to bring out as starkly as possible what is apparently being suggested here. For Derrida speculates that cruelty – the possibility of cruelty – is not merely the exclusive preserve of psychoanalysis, but that it is indispensable to life itself, irreducible to the living being in any form.

In all these examples, then, the meaning or sense cruelty acquires, however impossibly, is due to its juxtaposition or interrelationship with another term or set of terms (sovereignty, power, resistance, psychoanalysis, 'death drive, the aggression drive, or sadism, etc.', mutation, life itself, etc.) rather than through the possibility of an opposable term of the sort that Derrida suggests Freud may believe in. By page 271 of *Without Alibi*, more than thirty pages into his text, Derrida may thus be found to write:

> When I speak yet again, in the double wake of Nietzsche and Freud, of a cruelty that would have no contrary or that in any case would be irreducible, with the result that any contrary would have to compromise with it, I mean this: there are only differences in cruelty, differences in modality, quality, intensity, or reactivity within a *same* cruelty.

The very idea of the definition, delimitation or determination of the identity or meaning of a term by dint of *opposition* now seems to have been abandoned, and perhaps with good reason, given the preceding discussion – both Derrida's, and mine – of cruelty's complexity, doubleness and ambiguity. Indeed, in a seemingly endless procession of mutations which perhaps help define cruelty's spectacle, its perhaps indispensable theatricality (in which psychoanalysis, so Derrida hints, will have been a principal actor), 'politics' is added to the list of cruelty's doubles, since 'no politics will be able to eradicate it. Politics can only domesticate it, differ and defer it, learn to negotiate, compromise *indirectly*' (p. 252): that is, according to the very figure or motif – that of the 'indirect' – by which we are coming to recognise cruelty's very possibility. Law, too, enters the stage as another of cruelty's doubles, in the sense that the US Supreme Court's approval in the 1970s of a state ruling that lethal injection is not 'cruel'[10] in fact heaps cruelty upon cruelty, doubles cruelty with itself. Indeed, for Derrida this perhaps tops the list of cruelties included in the endless, bottomless archive of worldwide memory, being all the more 'obscene', 'unjust' and 'barbaric' – all the more 'cruel' – for the fact that it is apparently non-bloody or non-cruel (p. 266). Neither is ethics free from this irreducible ambiguity we are calling cruelty (p. 267). But then why does Derrida insist, right from the outset, on a possible distinction (or even an opposition of sorts) between Nietzsche and Freud, over the question of whether an 'opposable' or 'contrary' term can be anything more than a condition or consequence of the 'without-limit' or the *same* of cruelty itself?

One more for the list, an inventory that is perhaps dominated by none of the terms that constitute it (due no doubt to the strange logic of its very possibility): autoimmunity. The concepts of sovereignty and cruelty are inscribed by, or within, 'an ambiguity that is as unrelievable as autoimmunity itself', writes Derrida (p. 260). Cruelty is autoimmune, as is surely becoming apparent by now; yes, that's surely something we can be certain of . . .[11] What may be opposed to it is therefore perhaps nothing other than *itself*, cruelty itself as other-of-itself. Cruelty opposing itself as non-opposable or at any rate non-oppositional term. Cruelty inhering, in fact, in the profound contrariness that establishes its possibility, its self-relation. Cruelty itself, therefore, to be added to the interminable list of cruelty's doubles, as perhaps its ironic completion. Cruelty, in the end, including and dominating all its 'others' or 'doubles', in a movement by which it ultimately squares up to itself. Dominating itself, dominated by itself, dividing against itself, not quite adding up to itself as precisely 'itself': cruelty.

Still the question: given the irreducible ambiguity, duplicity or doubleness of cruelty (in apparently endless form), why, in his opening remarks, does Derrida maintain a potential schism between Nietzsche and Freud, highlighting the possibility of a dispute over the nature of what is 'opposable' or 'contrary', a possible disagreement over whether this can be anything other than a mere effect of the 'without-limit'? Is Derrida just guilty of a certain inconsistency or incoherence, as we move from the beginning of the essay towards its end, or is it that he just gives up on the 'opposable term' in anything other than its very weakest form (that is, as a function of the system which it resists only to encourage and intensify its cruelty all the more)? Within a page's space of Derrida's contention that there are only 'differences in modality . . . within a *same* cruelty', we get this:

> Indirection, the ruse of the detour (*Umweg*) consists, to put it too succinctly (but this is not the essential thing that concerns me here), in bringing into play the antagonistic force of Eros, love and love of life, against the death drive. There is thus a contrary to the cruelty drive, even if the latter knows no end. There is an opposable term, even if there is not a term that puts an end to the opposition. (p. 272)

The Freudian proposition is therefore not just abandoned, it is reasserted. But how so, exactly? To the extent that the death drive is in cahoots with cruelty, the 'antagonistic force of Eros, love and love of life' is, here, its contrary, its opposable term. And yet there is no term that puts an end to the opposition. Which one? The seeming opposition between life, love of life, and death, the death drive? This apparent opposition – this fight-to-the-death or fight-for-life, one might say – is, of course, perhaps the cruellest of all, since, without love of life, death or the death drive would surely be incapable of cruelty (a cruelty which may, of course, be done as much in the name of 'love of life' as anything else). Without love of life, death would presumably be incapable of being cruel, or – if the death-drive is essentially incapable of cruelty – of nevertheless inflicting cruelty, of causing cruelty to happen. Yet if cruelty therefore dominates the opposition between life and death – if it gives us the very term that hyphenates their relation, as it were – it cannot put an end to this same opposition. Cruelty cannot master it once and for all, cannot decisively overcome the forces within such an opposition that in fact remain hostile to cruelty (whether those of 'life or 'death'), not without putting itself to an end. No cruelty without love of life (whether or not such 'love' is, in essence, cruel or non-cruel), no cruelty without the forces of death (even if death is not itself essentially 'cruel'). Cruelty, as Derrida tells us, can in any event have no 'end', not merely in the sense that its irreducible gratuitousness exceeds any intended purpose, but in the sense that – as precisely its own contrary or duplicitous double – cruelty cannot be delimited or given in single form *by definition*. Such a thing would be terminal for cruelty itself. Thus cruelty and the 'opposable term', indeed the opposition itself, must and can only *survive* one another. Surviving one another, one might say, 'life' and 'death' can neither overcome their relation by resolving its antagonisms within a single identity, nor merely separate from one another in a static or stable binary. The diversion or delay, by which the opposable term is not just brutally mastered nor endlessly awaited but instead remarked otherwise and survived, is thus not *simply* cruel. Derrida has not simply been cruel in making us wait for the opposable term, since this detour or '*indirect* stratagem' may be akin to the form survival might take. Life itself is not merely cruel, always already cruel. It is also nothing less than the very survival *of* cruelty (double genitive again). As Derrida suggests in *For What Tomorrow*, a 'legal' end to the death penalty will not entail an end to the *possibility* of the death penalty or, for that matter, an end to all the deathly and cruel possibilities *by other means* that it entails or encapsulates. There will always be some death penalty, even if by another name; there will always be some cruelty, even if – and perhaps inevitably – by some other name.[12] Even if 'the disappearance of the death penalty' was 'just a change of modality', its abolition 'just another way of feeding a certain addiction to the love of humanity that allows the worst', as Olivia Custer has put it,[13] nevertheless the ceaseless cruelty undoubtedly done in the name of this 'love of humanity' as much as in the name of its opposite[14] (or, for that matter, in the name of that 'love' which, as Derrida puts it in 'For the Love of Lacan', 'has never needed the analytic situation to claim its victims') does not completely countermand or exhaust the resources of 'life' as they are doubled and divided between 'life-death' in the name of what I am calling 'survival *of* cruelty'. (Indeed, if 'life' for a certain Freud is in one sense the effect of what is inorganic, non-vital or inanimate, or of deathly or deadly drives, it is also and at the same time – and perhaps even without contradiction – precisely the *resistance* of such force, in the sense that force acquires its very force only through the possibilities of resistance, just as the effects of gravity take hold or become real only at the point gravity itself is resisted. If 'life' is therefore always and already trapped by the deadly machine that forms its origin, it is also – for perhaps the entire philosophical tradition in which psychoanalysis is caught up – the *resistance* of death/resistance *of* death. To note this complexity is not to seek a return to vitalist doctrines; it is rather to articulate the resistance or resistances *of* life in a way that complicates what we might mean by the purely machinic 'origin', or the absolute rule of death, reminding us that the latter does not have a single face, is as non-self-identical or divisible as 'life' itself.)

'Life', then, as the survival *of* cruelty – *Beyond the Pleasure Principle* taught us as much right from the start – this is perhaps the meaning of the schism between Nietzsche and Freud that Derrida wants to maintain from the very beginning (albeit by means of the detours and diversions that, as should now be obvious, are far from just a stylistic feature of his essay). For Derrida's Freud, cruelty-in-life is indeed 'endless but not without contrary' in the sense I have just proposed, and as such the resources of a psychoanalysis-still-to-come – a psychoanalysis impossibly beyond itself – attest to just this possibility of a survival of cruelty, which is also necessarily a survival of love and love of life itself as much as of death. As such, this thinking concerning the survival *of* cruelty in all forms of life should perhaps be taken, in its most rigorous sense, to provide a possible means to respond to the archive and spectacle of cruelty in all its unexampled instances – this, at any rate, might be one possible 'Freudian future' beyond Freud himself. And, for that matter, beyond a certain Lacan, for whom 'clinical treatment, institutionalized in a certain mode', not only authorised his dismissive assessment of Derrida and, thereby, the exclusion of deconstruction from the privileged scene of psychoanalysis, but transformed, as Derrida himself puts it, 'the rules governing the analytic situation into criteria of absolute competence for speaking'.[15]

Post-scriptum

In his reading of the work of Hélène Cixous, *H. C. for Life, That Is To Say . . .*[16] Derrida writes:

> If, as I suggest, life has no other side, if there is only one side, the one of living life, then the latter remains undecidable, certainly, since one does not have to decide and can no longer decide between two opposable edges or sides, but this undecidable is the place of decision which, however serious it may be, can only be *for life*. Because it is undecidable, one can decide and settle only for life. But life, which is undecidable, is also, in its very finitude, infinite. What has only one side – a single edge without an opposite edge – is infinite. Finite because it has an edge on one side, but infinite because it has no opposable edge. (pp. 47–8)

Since, here, 'life' has 'no other side', 'no opposable edge', does this mean that the status of the 'opposable term', upon which I have placed so much emphasis, is simply undermined by a basic incoherence that runs across or between these two texts by Derrida? Amid all the avowed complexity of the 'contrary' term, does a simple contradiction crop up here, with not inconsiderable irony? Does *H. C. for Life* – whether unintentionally or not – countermand 'life-death' as it is thought by Derrida in his essay on psychoanalysis, cruelty and the death penalty?

In *H. C. for Life*, Derrida insists that death is 'not denied' by Cixous, but nevertheless 'it is not a side, it is a nonside' (p. 52). Death is not merely something that is beyond all possible experience, that is absolutely unknowable, or even that is utterly unthinkable as such (these types of formulation in fact reinscribe death as not just a limit or edge, but as *something* beyond the limit or edge). Instead, for Derrida, strictly speaking death is more radically *impossible*, thus not attributable to the *place* of a 'side'. If there is no other side to life, beyond its own limit, ending or edge, this is what renders life 'in-finite' in its very finitude. Undecidable, in the sense that it is not determinable or delimitable according to the presence of a (non-complex) opposite term, paradoxically 'life' establishes the very conditions of decidability (any decision truly worthy of the name arises on condition not of what is decidable, what is already decided as decidable, but of what is undecidable in a more radical sense), although, since death is a 'nonside', one can only decide in terms of 'life', '*for life*', one way or the other – even if one decides to die. Thus, throughout life (even at the point of choosing death, which is a moment not just *in* life but *of* life), 'it is a question of life and not death, of a differential power of life over life that stays alive, keeps itself alive, comes back to life. There is no side to death, this is what finitude means, paradoxically; what comes around here, on this side . . . which is only the side of life, is living life' (p. 80).

In this same passage, however, Derrida observes:

> What decides here *for life* is not a wish for immortality or eternity, at least in the accepted sense of these words, which will therefore have to be swiftly changed in a moment. For this appellation, which catches the ghost by a wisp of life, there is a time of survival that is life itself, life in life (a life that is no more death than the opposite of death, a life that does not know death). (p. 81)

While both the mention of 'survival' as a recurring Derridean theme and the rebuttal of 'immortality or eternity, at least in the accepted sense' retain a certain consistency, once again 'life' is affirmed as neither the 'opposite' of death nor in relation to death *as such*: once more, the in-finity of life, or '*for life*', seems to depend on precisely such non-opposition (of which non-relation would be the expression or form). If death is a 'nonside', in other words, the question surely cannot be one of death opposed to life, life against death, or even life in exchange for death, life calculably extracted or subtracted from death as, for instance, countable remaining time: in another formulation, citing Cixous's *Jours de l'an*, Derrida's text calls upon us to think of death not as that which is *dead*, that which simply establishes the limit or end to life, but rather that which is alive, everywhere alive in life. But – as this very formulation itself testifies – nor is Derrida asking us simply to think of life *without* death, or even the *possibility* of life-without-death. A few pages later, he refers once more to 'this strange logic of the edge without an opposite edge, a unique side on the one hand [*d'un côté unique*], certainly, but not without another, quite the contrary'. Always and already 'turned to the other', 'held to the other' through and through, this is nonetheless 'a unique side without another side' – and this would be 'life itself', says Derrida (p. 52). For sure, 'death' may not be the only name for this other (which is not another 'side'); as a term, it may not exhaust without remainder the resources of the 'other'. Later in the text, however, Derrida insists that he does not want to say of the *'for life'* that

> a certain decomposable 'being-for' would be more originary than anything else, the absolute origin of meaning. No, before the being-for, and even the being-of-life-for, there would be the life-for-life, the for-life, which at once gives and replaces life with life in view. And this is why, up to the end, 'for life' has no end, it knows no end. Everything happens on the side of 'for,' but I have not yet done wandering along [*côtoyer*] this strange shore that one calls a side. This 'for life' is not a *being* for life symmetrically opposed to the famous *Sein zum Tode*, being-toward-death, as its other side. It is on the same side. (pp. 87–8)

Here, Derrida is not simply taking his distance from essentialist or onto-logical conceptions of life.[17] He is also arguing that since 'life' is in non-relationship to 'death' construed as simple, symmetrical opposite (that is, the adversarial *something* beyond 'life' itself), paradoxically 'death' is irreducible to the 'life', the *'for life'*, which exists in non-relation to it. ('It is on the same side'.) The power of the 'contrary' is here surely re-established at just the point a more simple opposition is denied: death pervades life in non-relation to it, thus splitting 'life', dividing it undecid-ably from and within itself, thus distributing it to itself and opposing it to itself in the same, divisible movement. This surely comes closer to the thinking of 'life-death' found in 'Psychoanalysis Searches the States of Its Soul' than the simple logic of contradiction – of which neither partake – would allow.

In the Epilogue to *H. C. for Life*, Derrida writes at last: 'Between her and me, it is as if it were a question of life and death. Death would be on my side and life on hers' (p. 158). A gracious irony to close with, perhaps, since death is, after all, a 'nonside', albeit one that remains – as *Jours de l'an* affirms – alive, in life, and in the *'for life'*. Life *and* death, like psychoanalysis *and* cruelty, a strange economy or aneconomy that supplements itself always with the other, an 'other' neither simply inside nor outside, dominating nor dominated, but instead always subject to the question of the side without another side still 'held to the other'. While in 'Psychoanalysis Searches the States of Its Soul' there is 'thus a contrary to the cruelty drive, even if the latter knows no end', in *H. C. for Life* we have 'this strange logic of the edge without an opposite edge

. . . but not without another, quite the contrary'. It is as if, here, the 'contrary' and the 'opposite' change places, or, rather, the 'contrary' comes back to take (spectral) possession of the absent 'opposite' in the latter text, just as the 'opposite' radicalises the force and meaning of the 'without-contrary' in the former one. And these highly non-simple relations – those of life-death, Cixous-Derrida, psychoanalysis *and* cruelty – point once more to the always divisible resources of a survival (survival of life-death) with which we must continue to reckon, however impossibly, however cruelly.

Notes

1. Jacques Derrida, 'For the Love of Lacan', in *Resistances of Psychoanalysis*, trans. Peggy Kamuf, Pascale-Anne Brault and Michael Naas (Stanford: Stanford University Press, 1998), p. 67.
2. Jacques Derrida, 'Psychoanalysis Searches the States of Its Soul: The Impossible Beyond of a Sovereign Cruelty', in *Without Alibi*, ed. and trans. Peggy Kamuf (Stanford: Stanford University Press, 2002), pp. 238–80. Further page references will be included in the main body of the chapter.
3. As Derrida observes in 'Psychoanalysis Searches the States of Its Soul', while cruelty may be 'assigned to its Latin inheritance, that is to a very necessary history of spilled blood (*cruor, crudus, credelitas*)' it may also be 'affiliated to other languages and other semantics' (including, importantly, Freud's German) in which what is cruel remains 'unrelated to the flow of blood', or is at least not essentially dependent on blood-spilling (pp. 238–9). If psychic (i.e. 'bloodless') cruelty is in some sense the 'proper' object of psychoanalysis, as Derrida starts to suggest, nevertheless his own writing, here and elsewhere (notably on the death penalty), works to unsettle the opposition between both the cruel and supposedly non-cruel and the bloody and bloodless, contaminating the borderlines which ostensibly divide them from one another. As Elizabeth Rottenberg claims, however, it is perhaps 'psychical, bloodless' cruelty that, for Derrida, makes cruelty so hard to delineate as such (and, therefore, so difficult to divide from 'bloody' cruelty), while making it at the same time the very horizon of psychoanalysis's resources. (See Elizabeth Rottenberg, 'Cruelty and Its Vicissitudes: Jacques Derrida and the Future of Psychoanalysis', *Southern Journal of Philosophy*, 50 (2012) (Spindel Supplement, 'Derrida and the Theologico-Political: From Sovereignty to the Death Penalty'): 143–59, esp. p. 154.)
4. For recent mutations in the practice of the death penalty in the United States, see Peggy Kamuf, 'Protocol: Death Penalty Addiction', *Southern Journal of Philosophy* , 50 (2012) (Spindel Supplement): 5–19. See also, in the same volume, Elizabeth Rottenberg, 'Cruelty and Its Vicissitudes', the latter pointing out that Derrida himself, in the interview with Elisabeth Roudinesco translated as *For What Tomorrow*, in fact used the word 'mutation' to describe important changes or modifications in the discourse and practice of the death penalty in the United States (see p. 145).
5. Sigmund Freud, *The Standard Edition of the Complete Psychological*

Works, Vol. VII, ed. James Strachey (London: Hogarth Press, 1957), pp. 123–245: see p. 160. Further page references will be included in the main body of the chapter.

6. For instance, in a note appended to the third part of 'A Case of Hysteria' (the section entitled 'The Second Dream'), Freud comments on the prominence, within the structure of the dream, of Dora's 'phantasy of revenge' against her father, 'which stands out like a façade in front of the rest', but which also stands for and includes a highly layered series of vengeful thoughts and actions. Freud concludes the note by stating, somewhat enigmatically: '– Cruel and sadistic tendencies find satisfaction in this dream'. (See *The Standard Edition of the Complete Psychological Works*, Vol. VII, pp. 110–11.)

7. See Gilles Deleuze, 'Coldness and Cruelty', in *Masochism* (New York: Zone Books, 1991), pp. 9–138, esp. the third section, 'Are Sade and Masoch Complementary?', pp. 37–6.

8. For Deleuze, the transition from masochistic to sadistic behaviour, or vice versa, indicates less their interchangeability or reversibility than a further expression of that which constitutes each, non-equivalent condition in the first place. This implicitly entails a different argument about cruelty's 'doubleness', notably at the moment of 'humorous' and 'ironic' change or transition that Deleuze identifies as a possible outcome of the masochistic and sadistic enterprise respectively.

9. On this point, see Elizabeth Rottenberg, 'Cruelty and Its Vicissitudes', p. 155.

10. As Kelly Oliver writes, the three-drug protocol that has been developed to administer the death penalty by lethal injection in the United States includes a second, muscle-paralysing drug which conceals suffering and thus allows the fiction or impression of humane or non-cruel killing. 'In other words', she writes, 'the three-drug protocol is designed to circumvent the very possibility of establishing whether or not the condemned man is suffering or in pain, whether or not his death is cruel or unusual.' Oliver goes on to note that, as Derrida himself observed, 'the word "cruel" comes from the Latin root *crudus*, which means rough, raw, or bloody, and shares its root with the word "crude". The crude or cruel death is one that is raw and bloody, not sterile and clean' (p. 92). In fact, as is noted by several contributors to the volume in which this essay appears, long before the adoption of lethal injection in the US, the use of the guillotine in revolutionary France was seen as progressive, egalitarian and thus, by some, as a certain departure in regard to more bloody forms of cruelty. Of course, the argument that proceeds from Derrida's 'Psychoanalysis Searches the States of Its Soul', as well as his other writings on the death penalty, entails a powerful deconstruction of all the oppositions between bloody and bloodless, humane and inhumane, cruel and non-cruel. (See Kelly Oliver, 'See Topsy "Ride the Lightning": The Scopic Machinery of Death', *Southern Journal of Philosophy*, 50 (2012) (Spindel Supplement): 74–94. On the three-drug protocol used in US executions, see also in this edition Peggy Kamuf, 'Protocol: Death Penalty Addiction', pp. 5–19. On cruelty, blood and the guillotine, see Elizabeth Rottenberg, 'Cruelty and Its Vicissitudes', p. 152.)

11. My tone here is partly aimed at the new-found dominance in Derrida

studies of the term 'autoimmunity', due to a number of recent texts including Martin Hägglund's *Radical Atheism: Derrida and the Time of Life* (Stanford: Stanford University Press, 2008), which have somewhat encouraged a rather unthinking affirmation and repetition of the word. Since I have referred several times to the previous Spindel Supplement of the *Southern Journal of Philosophy*, let me give an example of the near-pervasive spectre of autoimmunity. In his essay, 'Derrida on the Death Penalty', Matthais Fritsch writes that 'the structure of selfhood cannot be had without cruelty'. There would perhaps be several ways to interpret or develop this idea, but for Fritsch it consists in the fact that 'sovereignty or power of agency requires a welcoming gesture toward an alterity that, however, also threatens it with its demise . . . In affirming itself, the self affirms the other that it must also keep at arm's length' (p. 71). (See Matthais Fritsch, 'Derrida on the Death Penalty', *Southern Journal of Philosophy*, 50 (2012) (Spindel Supplement): 56–73.)

12. See Jacques Derrida and Elisabeth Roudinesco, *For What Tomorrow . . .: A Dialogue*, trans. Jeff Fort (Stanford: Stanford University Press, 2004), cited and discussed in Elizabeth Rottenberg, 'Cruelty and Its Vicissitudes', p. 146.

13. Olivia Custer, 'Angling for a Stranglehold on the Death Penalty', *Southern Journal of Philosophy*, 50 (2012) (Spindel Supplement): 160–73, esp. p. 163.

14. In *H. C. for Life*, trans. Laurent Milesi and Stefan Herbrechter (Stanford: Stanford University Press, 2006), Derrida writes: 'The *Rat Man* is nothing but a long development insisting on the fact that love does not extinguish hatred, quite the contrary, nor the care for life the death wish' (p. 109).

15. See Jacques Derrida, 'For the Love of Lacan', p. 67.

16. *H. C. for Life, That Is To Say . . .*, trans. Laurent Milesi and Stefan Herbrechter (Stanford: Stanford University Press, 2006). Further page references will be included in the main body of the chapter.

17. Later in the text, Derrida suggests that the question of '*for life*' goes before 'any philosophical, scientific or cultural thesis on being as life or on the essence of the living. It is not an ontology of life . . .' (p. 114).

Chapter 6

Grief-substitutes, or,
Why Melanie Klein Is So Funny

'Ideas come to us as the substitutes for grief' (Proust)

For Melanie Klein, there is no psychic condition that can be character-ised in terms of an objectless state, or in other words there is no psychic experience without an object. As Julia Kristeva – one of Klein's most critically astute readers – puts it, for her *'object-relations are at the centre of emotional life'*.[1] However, this very same relationality gives rise to 'object' anxiety from the outset. Such anxiety, focused on the mother's breast as exemplary, takes particular forms: fear of persecu-tion, the projection of destructive impulses, a desire to raid what is 'good' and violently exteriorise what is 'bad' about the now-split object (wherein such violent intention may manifest itself, nevertheless, in terms of the wish to *consume* the 'other'), and so on. Thus, the Kleinian breast is constituted, in Kristeva's terms, as an *'amalgam* of representa-tions . . . a diverse array of internal objects' (pp. 63–4), the ambivalence of which is reflected in the instability of psychic identity as it develops. To raid the 'good' contents of the other, as the obverse of sadistic wishes, is of course also a form of self-harm. If psychic life is intrinsically object-related, then to split the other – albeit in the interests of defend-ing the ego against its 'object' – is also to split the self. Thus, as Kristeva observes, the 'good' breast as much as the 'bad' is 'laden with traps' (p. 67). These specific effects of 'object anxiety' are exemplified by what Klein terms the paranoid-schizoid position, found typically in infants of under six months old. Here, the psychic condition of the child is in con-stant danger of disintegration – or, rather, it is defined or 'positioned' by such disintegration itself, the ego taking its self-protective form only in terms of fragmenting projections (for instance, through projecting onto a particular outside, splitting off a 'bad' part of oneself that the other also is, or, alternatively, feeling devalued or lessened in the ideal pres-ence of the 'good' object with which one wishes, however impossibly, to identify, and thereby losing primacy as such[2]). What is needed, therefore, is the capacity to recognise or assume the deep-seated ambivalence of one's drives, to be able to synthesise what has become split, to stabilise one's relationship to both the other and the self. If projective identification underlies psychotic structures, it also constitutes an initial stage of bonding with the world, a sort of psychic 'exhalation', or outward-expression, as Kristeva, following Florence Guignard, puts it (p. 71). This outer-directedness establishes the possibility of another psychic position, visible from the age of about six months onwards. Here, the child develops the ability to conceive of the 'whole' object and thereby the 'self' as an integrated entity. Or, rather, the infant more specifically acquires the capacity to experience the *loss* of the object as a whole. Whether this is due to neurobiological maturation involving stronger syntheses in perception and memory or other psychic mechanisms, the move away from the paranoid-schizoid position is therefore allied to the situation of mourning. The degree of splitting is diminished only to the extent that the new psychic position allows full loss of the other as 'loved one' (such 'love' being defined through its capacity to take the 'good' with the 'bad', as it were). This introjection of the 'whole' other, the complete person, lays the ground for the ego to experience its own integration, to limit its reliance upon fracturing projections, violent separations and malformed objects. Nonetheless, such psychic gain comes at the price not just of a differently difficult situation, but also of a fresh understanding of one's reliance upon the other as both a 'total' and a complex object. The ambivalence towards the other that must be assumed remains far from unproblematic, making new demands upon the 'self', new jealousies and anxieties arise, while the developing ego is beset by the onset of guilt for earlier destructive impulses of which it is now ashamed. All of this characterises what Klein calls the depressive position. It may lead to mania or, perhaps more gradually, reparation – which in turn encourages creativity as an expression of the desire to make good. Nevertheless, those psychic defences once directed towards the object as a source of persecution are not so much liberated (set free from the violent terrors of the 'bad' object or the oppressive ideality of the 'good') as they are turned towards depressive and remorseful anxiety. The depressive position may be less fluid and divisive for the ego, but nonetheless the Kleinian subject is still, in Kristeva's formidable phrase, 'founded upon a dynamic of abjection whose optimal quality is fascination' (p. 72). Making (creative) reparation to objects is far from idyllic, tinged as it is with desperate remorse – for it cannot be forgotten that the object was once put into pieces, and is now capable only of (mournful) repair. Reparation, in other words, always includes the anxious memory of disintegration, of the destructive aggression that founds one's relation to the object of one's love, and so on (however submerged this memory may be).

For a thinker like D. W. Winnicott, much influenced by Klein, likening the relationship of the psychotic-schizoid and depressive positions to the distinction Woody Allen draws between the 'horrible' and the 'miserable' might be to downplay the healthy aspects of the depressive position as a normal part of development. (In *Annie Hall*, Allen's character says 'the horrible are like, I don't know, terminal cases, you know, and blind people, crippled. I don't know how they get through life. It's amazing to me. And the miserable is everyone else. So you should be thankful that you're miserable'.) Winnicott argues that 'the term "depressive position" is a bad name for a normal process', creating the impression of illness. He goes so far as to suggest that the depressive position should not be confused with the sense of depression at all.[3] Yet Allen's rather doleful evocation of the 'miserable' is, for all that, also an evocation of the 'normal'. In contrast to the terrifyingly 'horrible' (which, through its associations with crippling disability or blindness does convey some sense of the disintegrative and near-terminally destructive aspects of paranoid-schizoid psychosis), the 'miserable' comes as . . . something of a relief. Its sheer mundaneness is no doubt depressing but nonetheless far from purely desolating – although seemingly only if the 'horrible' is (as in *Annie Hall*) brought to mind rather than simply repressed. The sense of the 'miserable' as an everyday source of misery and relief alike – indeed, of gratitude, too ('you should be thankful that you're miserable') – does seem distinctly Kleinian. Yet as Kristeva points out, what is perhaps more interesting about the depressive position is that, by generating the resources for language and thinking (grounded in the capacity for the symbolisation of an object), it confirms Proust's contention that 'ideas come to us as the substitutes for griefs' (p. 77).[4] Here, albeit from a very different starting point, we find another echo of Lyotard's notion that, for a certain Kant, thought *is* pain. (We also glimpse, perhaps, another way to answer Rancière's notion of mourning as simply abnormally paralysing, not least since in Klein mourning and creative inventiveness seem as closely linked as 'griefs' are to 'ideas'.)[5] Proust continues (although this part of the passage is not quoted by Kristeva): '. . . and griefs, at the moment when they change into ideas, lose some part of their power to injure our heart; the transformation itself, even, for an instant, releases suddenly a little joy'.[6] What is interesting here is that the transformation of griefs into ideas – what Kristeva would see as the Kleinian transition from the paranoid-schizoid to the depressive position – involves, paradoxically, the very division of grief, its reduction by a part or in part, so that the creation of a more integrated ego would still seem to be founded on the capacity to separate or split, which – in a split-second or instant – establishes in turn the possibility of 'joy'. This splitting of time as much as of founding grief as the basis for such joy is no doubt troubling to Proust's conception of the idea, to the extent that he is quick to add a qualification that is also a reversal of sorts: 'But substitutes only in the order of time, for the primary element, it seems, is the idea, and grief is merely the mode in which certain ideas make their first entry into us.'[7] In other words, ideas substitute for or replace griefs only in terms of a temporal order characterised by a more or less reductive chronology, while more fundamentally ideas 'constitute the primary element', the essence which griefs convey as 'merely' a 'mode' of their expression. On the basis of a comparison with the psychic positions she wished to elaborate, it seems likely that Klein would dispute this qualification as strongly as she might endorse its constituting or prior proposition. If it is a qualification that Kristeva sets apart in order to confirm the Proustian connection of Klein's thought, its reincorporation or recollection here far from reintegrates the Proustian text itself. Amid these somewhat pained relations of splitting and synthesis, the unreconciled nature of the depressive position – indeed, the unreconciled origin of 'ideas' in 'griefs' – perhaps re-emerges once more. (Here, among other technical distinctions and complications of 'part' and 'whole', the ambivalence of the term 'substitute' should not be overlooked.)

Laugh-Out-Loud Loneliness (Loneliness Out-lives . . .)

Among Klein's very last writings is her essay 'On the Sense of Loneliness'.[8] This dwells not upon any particular experience of being deprived of company, but on a more deep-seated 'inner sense of loneliness' that may still persist despite the presence of friends or loved ones. Klein attributes this to the impossible yet tenacious longing for a 'perfect internal state' which may be experienced by schizophrenics (those whose psychic position in relation to their 'objects' still leaves them 'dominated by splitting mechanisms' and thus struggling against excessive disintegration), depressives (who despite a measure of egoistic integration and cohesion necessarily retain the guilt-ridden memory of divisive aggressivity and destructiveness), and thus, of course, 'to some extent . . . everyone' (p. 99), whether ill or not. (Indeed, the impossibility of such a 'perfect internal state' occurs to the self at the point at which, in the move to the depressive position, it understands and accepts that 'the good object can never approximate to the perfection expected from the ideal one' (p. 105), bringing about a general 'de-idealisation' which affects the self's experience of itself as much as its conception of the other. Yet according to Klein the glamorous dream of such perfection is never quite given up, retaining a certain necessity in psychic life.)

Early on in the essay Klein suggests that a 'satisfactory early relation to the mother' is based upon 'close contact' operating at the level of the unconscious – both that of the parent and the child. This intimacy, then, is avowedly 'preverbal', and as such it predates the acquisition of language, or the ability to express thoughts, that comes with the capacity for symbolisation. Thus 'an understanding without words' (p. 100), as Klein puts it, is perhaps the closest one might come to an ideal state – while at the same time, of course, it is only through the attainment of what may be termed language in its broadest sense that a pathway to creative and reparative development is opened later on in psychic life. The terrible irony, therefore, is that one yearns for the very same condition or situation which, in order to acquire a measure of normalcy or well-being, one must forgo. In this form the self is divided from itself anew, paradoxically by both the desire and demand for cohesion, by a dreamt-of wholeness that stretches back into an irretrievable past and forward into an unattainable future. This, for Klein, is the origin of a loneliness that cannot be overcome by the presence of others, not least since those others as objects of the ego cannot but participate or feature in the drama of 'object-relations' that constitutes the elaborate psychic dynamics of such loneliness in the first place.

In typically Kleinian fashion, within a paragraph's space we are told that insofar as it may ever have existed, the 'happy relation with the mother' would never have been 'undisturbed'. Beset by both the trauma of natality, or born life, and the destructive impulses unleashed by the death instinct, the infant is bound to fall prey to the 'persecutory anxiety' that arises at the prospect of the mother's breast. Once more, then, it is in the very midst of an ostensibly harmonious, intimate situation (rather than through its mere withdrawal) that loneliness arises. In these circumstances, the simple presence or absence of the other is somewhat beside the point, since one is just as lonely – or just as capable of loneliness – whether one is with or without them. To go further, loneliness is only made possible by the other as object of the ego, albeit that projective identification deeply complicates the nature of the other's 'externality', which for all that cannot be dominated by the primacy of the 'self', as we have already seen. (Indeed, the other as object of the ego may be as much a past or future 'self' as a present or absent friend, loved one or enemy.) Thus there is no loneliness without the other – whether that other is outside or within me. (As is obvious by now, this is far from simply a 'choice', either for the subject or critically, that is to say in terms of psychic theorisation.)

No more than its precursor, the depressive position offers little guarantee against the onset of loneliness. To offset destructive impulses, the move towards integration brings not only the capacity to incorporate the other as a whole, and to thereby stabilise the 'self' through attaining a measure of cohesion; it also produces the anxiety that, as one takes the 'good' with the 'bad', aggressivity may persist in threateningly intimate proximity to loving feelings, and that the 'good' object may therefore be as much endangered as preserved by integration. Or, to put a different slant on it, that the possibility of omnipotence on the part of the ego is jeopardised by the more complex 'reality' of relationality itself. Once more, intimate connection (in its highly ambivalent forms) rather than 'simple' desolating severance or profound non-belonging is traced at the origins of loneliness. As Klein puts it, 'I have heard patients express the painfulness of integration in terms of feeling lonely and deserted, through being completely alone with what to them was a bad part of the self' (p. 101). One is never alone (with) / one is always alone (with): this is perhaps the very structure of loneliness insofar as it describes the 'dynamic of abjection' that accompanies the always non-objectless or object-ridden Kleinian universe. To be free of pain is neither to be free of the other, nor is it to consummate or join the other. And since, at any rate, neither are possible in any simple sense (any more than, as desires or demands, they are simply avoidable – or any more than it might make sense to hope for freedom *from* the 'self'), to be free of pain is just not one of the options. Indeed, since the impossibility of full integration is also the impossibility of 'complete understanding and acceptance of one's own emotions' (p. 102), as Klein puts it, loneliness persists. The trouble with the Allenesque mantra 'you should be thankful that you're miserable' is that it's impossible to know just how miserable you truly are, and therefore to be sufficiently grateful about it. Which, given the Kleinian emphasis on guilt and reparation, is only bound to make things worse (though funnier, too). So it is in precisely the sense that one cannot commune with one's misery or loneliness (or: one can never make full reparation, one does not truly know what one is guilty of, since such guilt is – in part – on the part of the other-in-me), that one cannot be free of it. And yet at the same time it is the inextricable intimacy, the inseparable proximity of one's loneliness – a closeness that cannot finally be put into words, cannot be delimited, demarcated, or objectified as such – that intensifies lonely feelings. When Klein suggests of loneliness in a group-context that through projective identification the lost or split-off parts of the 'self' may be 'felt to be lonely' (p. 102), she might equally be talking about the loss of self-possession that happens in one's own company as much as in the company of other people. The two are not entirely separate, of course, in the way that they can confront us with the separation of the self from itself, forcing us to encounter our own self-alienation.

Is there a dark humour in some of Klein's writings, whether intentional or not?[9] (Derived from the Greek, Melanie means blackness or darkness.) Sentences which begin, for example: 'When paranoid anxiety is relatively strong, though still within the range of normality . . .' surely provoke us to laugh darkly? 'If, however, the ego is very weak, which I consider to be an innate feature . . .' (pp. 102–3) – ditto, surely? Are such constructions Allenesque in their drily despondent tone, coming close to litotes? (In *Manhattan*, Allen doesn't react to the contested notion of the benefits of parenting in a lesbian couple simply by exploding with an overgeneralisation: 'But no-one survives their mothering!' Instead, the enhanced comic effect comes from the more moderately or negatively phrased: 'I always feel very few people survive one mother'.) To understate for emphasis surely has something to do with the psychic life Klein describes, which is painful to excess precisely because of both its resolutely modest accomplishments and the sheer mundaneness of its failings – a rather pathetic yet recurrent drama of partial losing and semi-regaining. It is the very ordinariness of both – matched, perhaps, by the matter-of-factness of Klein's tone – that is so funny. Funny, however, because it is set against the always-impending backdrop of what seems truly awful, although funnier than Allen, as I've already suggested, because such awfulness can never be truly appreciated. It is as if constraint itself provokes the exorbitance of laughter, as if putting the mockers on an excess so inordinate that it could never, in any case, appear *as such* provokes the outburst by other means. One laughs, then, as much at the psychic condition Klein describes as at her own descriptions; one laughs not just at the other, but at oneself, as a deep form of participation in what is so funny. But of course this is only ever a partly 'knowing' participation, just as the form which occasions it must be under- rather than overstated. If many would not immediately recognise Klein as a humorous writer – Klein herself included, perhaps – let us not assume this reduces the potential for comic effect, far from it. The combination of inseparable proximity and estranging heterogeneity that we find here means that laughter is always a lonely business, something Klein knew not a little about.

What, then, mitigates loneliness? Klein gives several examples. If the ego is relatively strong, and a 'good early relation to the primal object' exists, the good breast can be internalised in the interests of a degree of integration that offsets loneliness's worst effects (p. 111). This comparatively successful internalisation may strengthen not only the image of the (m)other, but that of the self, thereby reducing aggressive and destructive impulses, promoting 'love' and indeed diminishing 'the harshness of the superego' with a view to less troubling object-relations on the part of the ego. The 'greater adaptation to reality' potentialised by the depressive position creates the possibility of 'an acceptance of one's own shortcomings', so that frustration or resentment can be lessened, and enjoyment of the world can be enhanced somewhat. Enjoyment, says Klein, goes hand in hand with gratitude, since the latter stimulates reparative-creative behaviour, prompting forms of generosity or giving that reinforce a positive sense of 'self'. Of course, gratitude is also in part a reaction to, or mixed up with, negative feelings such as guilt and envy – something Klein does not say here, but which she well appreciated. What she does say, however, is the following: 'The capacity for enjoyment is also the precondition for a measure of resignation which allows for pleasure in what is available . . .' (p. 112). This is another of those sentences that makes me laugh out loud, and for just the same reasons. With pure understatement, we are told that the capacity for enjoyment so crucial to our sense of well-being, and a key weapon in the struggle against loneliness, is always bound up with a sense of resignation that this world's pleasures will necessarily be limited, partly disappointing and probably brief. Even the mitigation of loneliness is described by Klein in terms, or rather in a form, that connects to the dark comedy of loneliness itself. Guilt may not overtly taint the value of gratitude promoted in these passages of Klein's essay, but loneliness returns in understated (comic) form – all the more powerful for that, perhaps – in order to moderate the very enjoyment that wishes away lonely feelings. Moderate enjoyment lessens resentfulness . . . maybe, but its very idea triggers a comic outburst (born of understatement) of just the kind that re-marks the lonely situation. It is perhaps not surprising, therefore, that after her brief set of comments about ameliorating loneliness, we are reminded rather baldly that lonely feelings can never entirely be eliminated. Here, though, the tone shifts from that of drily comic possibility (whether intentional or not) to a heavy solemnity deprived even of the comic potential of bathos. A full or final acceptance of loneliness is just not funny – this is ironic, perhaps, but it is necessarily so. What is so funny about loneliness is that we *can't* take its measure, that its understatement is always, paradoxically, extreme, an outburst as much as a constraint. Loneliness is funny, is comedy itself,[10] only as long as one isn't entirely sure what one is laughing at or for. And so (whether or not to be funny) Melanie embarks once again on her description of the various ways in which loneliness can be reduced or defended against, each one being at the same time the very cause of loneliness itself (heightened dependence on the mother, semi-delusional flight to the internal object, the approbation of the other, nostalgic recollection in old age, youthful idealisation of the future, the quest for independence and diminution of the need for love, and so on). Hilarious though this may seem, things nevertheless seem to get less funny as the list goes on, as if through the proliferation of examples the paradoxical case or situation of loneliness is being somehow overstated. Indeed, if it is *for all that* hardly stated at all, that is because the irony is by now all too obvious. The joke has gone on too long. Since birth, in fact from the very beginning, as Melanie here reminds us, perhaps with joke-saving timeliness. ('The first powerful impact . . . accompanies birth' (p. 114): unstatable exor- bitance, preverbal outburst.) Like the 'recurrent experiences of losing and regaining' that for Klein characterise 'early emotional life' (p. 104), the joke (of loneliness) is won and lost, lost and won again. It never enjoys the simple victory of the punchline, but instead extends before and after itself, being always and never quite timely. Once more, the essay stumbles into theoretical repetitiveness, and then is gone. Published posthumously, and so always questionable as the definitive version of itself, it appears as much before as after its time. Divided between an ever-departed origin and the unknowable horizon to come, perhaps tired of its own joke for company, it is itself lonely. Loneliness, as Klein concludes, is powerful enough to remain 'throughout life' – one last understatement, since as her essay shows true loneliness remains beyond us, outlives us, is perhaps all that outlives us.

But this can be put another way. What may outlive us, even and espe- cially as they signal the death-in-us, is precisely our reparative-creative works. In 'Infantile Anxiety Situations Reflected in a Work of Art and in the Creative Impulse',[11] written several decades earlier, early sadistic impulses directed toward the parent are analysed by way of the elabora- tion of the infant's sense of danger in terms of an 'anxiety situation' susceptible to psychoanalysis. The analytic scene here is the libretto written by Colette for Ravel's *L'enfant et les sortilèges*, the influence, obviously, Freud's. The projection of destructive wishes corresponds to the extreme sense of threat experienced by the child, but through the pleasure in destruction those maltreated things that convey certain human representations strangely come to life. Objects live. Broken crockery begins to jabber, torn wallpaper 'sounds a heart-breaking lament' as if it were the very 'rent fabric of the world' (p. 85), mathematical instruments abused during a much-resented lesson are transformed into a perplexing dancing figure, 'the spirit of mathematics' (p. 86). Furniture inside the house and the small animals just outside spring into anthropomorphised action. In short, the child has created a world with which to convey sadistic resentments, but also, ultimately, with which to sympathise, or at any rate to 'pity' (p. 89). This world, which in its domestic context is for Klein an expression of the mother's persecutory body, is within an initially hostile natural setting suddenly transformed so as to provide the circumstances for reparation to be made to the mother ('"That's a good child, a very well-behaved child," sing the animals' in response to the child's astonished whisper, 'Mama' (p. 86)). Thus, as this world comes to life, the attack directed on his parents (ink spilt in childish defiance of mathematical learning represents excremental soiling, the sharp shards of broken objects represent both the penis and that which may threaten it, and so forth) is converted in reparative terms into a scene of 'love'. The anxiety situation that provokes sadistic aggression also permits destructiveness of a creative and transformative kind. Rather like Deleuze's masochist, the child actively seeks, indeed deliberately provokes, punishment only so that he may play out his transgressive wishes with full licence, with a view here to addressing the anxiety creatively. It may not turn out quite as he expected – the control of the masochistic contract hardly seems in place – but nonetheless the gentle or 'loving' chastisement that replaces the more severe reprisals one might expect from such a wanton scene of destruction both fulfils the desire for reprimand and lessens anxiety into the bargain. Klein brings the story up a little short, however. Reparation as the other side of guilt never comes without the possibility of further 'disturbance', as she might well have put it. The world of objects brought to life by creative negotiation with one's own infantile anxiety may just as quickly revert to its original persecutory form. This, indeed, is the fragile and precarious condition of any relief the ego may obtain. Animated by human projections, the half-living things may enjoy a zombie afterlife, surviving beyond the scene of love and reparation that they occasion, making possible more complex relations that outlive the ego's attempt to thwart the forces of destruction. If, as in the tale Klein subsequently tells of the reparative value of painting in the case of Ruth Kjär, works of art may creatively address anxiety, including infantile guilt and the anxiety of loneliness, it is nevertheless also in this sense that our creative works (works like Klein's essay on loneliness, perhaps) may outlive us.

Notes

1. Julia Kristeva, *Melanie Klein* (New York: Columbia University Press, 2001). See especially pp. 57ff. Further page references will be given in the main body of the chapter.
2. The complexity is here compounded in the sense that, as one moves towards the depressive position, the realisation occurs that 'the good object can never approximate to the perfection of the ideal one' (p. 105), as Klein puts it in her essay 'On the Sense of Loneliness' (which this chapter will go on to discuss in more detail). This realisation is painful in that it brings to an end – or at any rate to a situation of crisis – the hope for a perfect or ideal 'self', thus creating the conditions for loneliness as they are described by Klein.
3. See D. W. Winnicott, 'The Depressive Position in Normal Emotional Development', in *Collected Papers* (London: Tavistock, 1955), pp. 264–5. In this context, it may also be interesting to note that Kristeva sees Klein's essay on loneliness as entering into a conversation with Winnicott's text, 'The Capacity to be Alone', which first appeared in 1958. Once more, in something of a contrast to the tone of Klein's essay, this text tends to stress the positive rather than negative dimensions of the capacity to be alone. Winnicott's essay can be found in his book *The Maturational Processes and the Facilitating Environment: Studies in the Theory of Emotional Development* (New York: International Universities Press, 1965).
4. Kristeva here cites from Marcel Proust, *In Search of Lost Time*, trans. Andreas Mayor and Terence Kilmartin, revised by D. J. Enright (London: Chatto & Windus, 1992), Vol. 6, *Time Regained*, p. 268.
5. This might include political inventiveness, including that of the left.
6. The subsequent section of the passage I quote here is also from this page in Proust, cited above (see note 4).
7. Ibid.
8. This essay can be found in Klein's book, *Our Adult World and Other Essays* (London: Heinemann, 1963), pp. 99–116. Page references will be given in the main body of the chapter.
9. In an interview given just a few years before her own death, Hanna Segal, a follower of Klein and a practising psychoanalyst who underwent analysis with her, described Klein as 'very good fun. She had a good sense of humour.' See 'Memories of Melanie Klein: an interview with Hanna Segal', which can be downloaded at http://www.melanie-klein-trust.org.uk/domains/melanie-klein-trust.org.uk/local/media/downloads/Memories_of_Melanie_Klein_Hanna_Segal.pdf.
10. Despite all of its temptations, one would need to be wary here of drifting into the old overgeneralisation which sees all comics – outwardly companionable though they may be – as ultimately depressed loners, although of course this same cliché might well establish the pretext for more rigorous analysis.
11. This essay, first published in 1929, can be found in *The Selected Melanie Klein*, ed. Juliet Mitchell (London: Penguin, 1986), pp. 84–94. Page references will be given in the main body of the chapter.

Index